BLOOM & PROFIT

HOW TO BUILD A PROFITABLE FLORAL
BUSINESS—AND ENJOY YOUR LIFE AGAIN

CHRISTI LOPEZ

SMART GROWTH BOOKS

Printed in the United States of America

ISBN: 979-8-9996713-0-1

Cover Design by Christi Lopez

Interior Design by Smart Growth Books

Published by Smart Growth Books

❀ Formatted with Vellum

CONTENTS

INTRODUCTION

Your Art Is Beautiful—But Is It Profitable? You Were Meant for More Than Just Scraping By.

You didn't start your floral business to struggle. You started it because flowers light you up. Because you love the way petals tell stories, the way arrangements bring joy, the way your artistry makes the world more beautiful.

And yet, here you are—working endless hours, pouring everything into your designs, and still wondering why your bank account doesn't reflect your talent.

Deep down, you *know* you were meant for more. More financial stability. More dream clients who truly value your work. More freedom to design without stress.

But let's be honest—right now, you feel stuck. You're afraid that if you raise your prices, clients will leave. That if you focus on business, you'll lose your creativity. That marketing will make you feel like a pushy salesperson.

I get it. I've been there. And I'm here to tell you: It doesn't have to be this way.

The florists who *thrive* aren't just the ones with the most talent.

They're the ones who learn to think like entrepreneurs. Who master pricing, marketing, and branding. Who stop playing small and start building a business that *works for them*, not the other way around.

This book is your blueprint. Inside, you'll learn how to price with confidence, attract high-end clients without feeling "salesy," and build systems that free up your time—so you can finally create a floral business that blooms right alongside your passion.

The Starving Artist vs. The Thriving Floral CFO

Let's talk about two florists. Maybe you know them. Maybe you *are* one of them.

The Starving Artist Florist:

- Creates breathtaking arrangements but struggles to charge what they're worth.
- Feels guilty raising prices and terrified of losing customers.
- Works 12+ hour days, trying to do *everything* alone.
- Posts on social media when they "have time" (which isn't often).
- Wakes up at 3 AM, worrying about cash flow.

The Thriving Floral CEO:

- Prices for profit—without apology.
- Attracts high-end clients who *respect* their artistry.
- Works smarter, not harder, with systems and automation.
- Markets their brand effortlessly—without feeling "salesy."
- Has financial security and *time* to enjoy life.

What makes the difference? *Mindset and strategy.* And that's exactly what this book is here to teach you.

From "Cottage Florist" to Multi-Six-Figure Floral CEO

I didn't start out as a business mogul. I was a passionate florist working out of my mom's basement—though I prefer the term "Cottage Florist," not Basement Betty, thank you very much! I was driven, creative, and deeply committed. But I had no business strategy. I overworked, undercharged, and ran my business on pure hustle.

Eventually, I made the bold leap to buy a struggling flower shop. I poured everything I had into turning it around—and I did. I built it into a thriving, seven-figure business with multiple locations.

Over the years, I weathered **three major economic downturns**, including 9/11, each one threatening to pull the rug out from under me. But I stayed the course. I leaned into **resilience** when things got hard, **tenacity** when the odds felt overwhelming, and **adaptability** when the market changed faster than I expected.

However, the pivotal moment occurred when I shifted my perspective from being solely a florist to becoming an entrepreneur. That mindset shift changed everything—from how I priced and marketed to how I led my team, served my clients, and scaled with intention.

Now I help florists like you make that same transformation—so you can stop just surviving and start truly thriving.

The Biggest Lies Keeping You Stuck (And What to Believe Instead)

Lie #1: "If my flowers are beautiful enough, customers will come."

Truth: Beautiful work is great—but *business* skills turn beauty into profit.

Lie #2: "Raising prices will scare away my customers."

Truth: The *right* customers *expect* to pay for quality.

Lie #3: "I have to do everything myself to succeed."

Truth: Smart florists automate, delegate, and build systems that free up time.

Lie #4: "Marketing is icky and salesy."

Truth: Marketing is storytelling—helping people fall in love with *you*.

Lie #5: "I'll always be overworked and underpaid."

Truth: You can create a floral business that *works for you* (not the other way around).

What This Book Will Teach You

This isn't just a business book. It's a *blueprint* for turning your floral passion into a thriving, sustainable business—without losing your creative spark. Inside, you'll learn:

✔ **Pricing Like a Pro** – How to confidently charge what you're worth (and get it).

✔ **Magnetic Marketing** – How to attract dream clients without feeling "salesy."

✔ **Business Systems That Save You Time** – So you can *finally* stop working 24/7.

✔ **Scaling Without Burnout** – How to grow without losing your sanity.

✔ **How to Become an In-Demand Floral Brand** – So customers seek *you* out.

This book isn't about "corporate" business advice. It's about giving you the tools, strategies, and confidence to *finally* create the floral business—and life—you deserve.

Your Business Is Your Masterpiece

Floristry is an art. But the real magic happens when you master the *business* of floristry. That's when you stop feeling like a struggling artist and start living like a thriving floral CEO.

Next Steps:

Take a deep breath and turn the page. Your transformation from struggling artist to thriving floral entrepreneur starts now.

Let's make your passion profitable.

1

THE FLORIST'S IDENTITY CRISIS: ARE YOU AN ARTIST OR AN ENTREPRENEUR?

I f you're holding this book, chances are you started your floral business because you love flowers, not spreadsheets. You likely dreamed of a life filled with beauty, creativity, and the joy of making people smile with your arrangements. But at some point, you realized something frustrating: talent alone isn't enough. Creativity doesn't automatically translate into profit. And now, here you are, wondering how to turn your passion into a thriving business. Welcome to the journey of becoming both an artist *and* an entrepreneur.

The Business, Not the Flowers, Is the True Art of Floristry

Many florists believe that creating arrangements is the most creative aspect of their work. However, what is the reality? The florists who succeed have developed a new form of artistic talent: **the art of business.**

Creating a flower brand, setting prices wisely, and doing marketing well are all creative endeavors. They call for creativity, vision, and intuition. Additionally, with the correct attitude and approach, you may become an expert in business, just as in floral design.

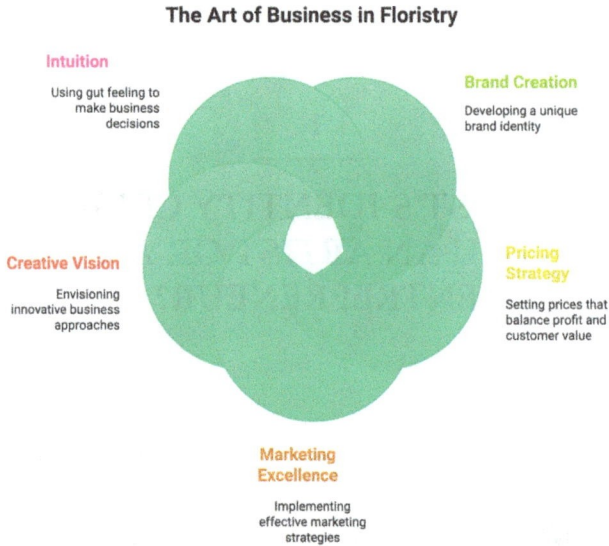

The Art of Business in Floristry

Intuition

Using gut feeling to
make business
decisions

Brand Creation

Developing a unique
brand identity

Creative Vision

Envisioning
innovative business
approaches

**Pricing
Strategy**

Setting prices that
balance profit and
customer value

**Marketing
Excellence**

Implementing
effective marketing
strategies

The Day I Almost Quit

I remember the morning vividly. I was sitting on a crate in the back of my flower shop, surrounded by buckets of blooms and piles of paper-work. My apron was soaked. My hands were dry and stained by lily pollen; my nails were dirty. My phone buzzed nonstop, and I had already skipped lunch—for the third day in a row.

It was supposed to be my dream job. Instead, I felt like I was drowning in a business I had built with my own hands.

Clients were happy, yes. The designs were beautiful. And behind the scenes? I was pricing blindly, juggling way too much, and struggling to pay myself consistently. I didn't need more flower knowledge. I needed a business blueprint. I needed clarity. I needed a path that didn't require burning out to succeed.

That's when I made the decision: I would no longer build my business on hustle. I would build it on **strategy**.

So I started studying what made businesses—not just flower

shops—truly thrive. I implemented systems, set boundaries, learned to price for profit, and—most importantly—began treating myself as the **CEO** of my business, not just its most exhausted employee.

That shift didn't just save my business. It saved me and others I've worked with now. And it led me here—to this book, to this movement, to **Bloom & Profit.**

Why Some Florists Struggle While Others Thrive

Let's talk about two types of florists:

1. The Starving Artist Florist

- She's wildly creative but struggles to price her work appropriately.
- She relies on word-of-mouth and resents social media marketing.
- She views business tasks as soul-sucking and ignores them until they become urgent problems.
- She never raises her prices because she's afraid of losing customers.

2. The Thriving Floral Entrepreneur

- She sees business as a creative challenge, not a burden.
- She prices for *profit*, not just for sales.
- She markets her work with confidence and attracts dream clients.
- She has systems in place that free up her time for creativity.

What makes the difference? **Mindset.** The florists who thrive aren't necessarily the most talented designers—they're the ones who embrace the *business* of flowers. It's what I call the "Bloom Mindset Shift". It's the transformation from artist to entrepreneur.

Focus on Art

May limit business
growth despite
artistic talent

**Embrace
Business**

Leads to thriving
business and
entrepreneurial
success

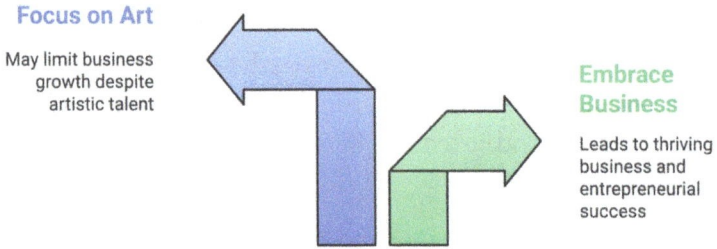

Case Study: Lewis Miller's Flower Flash

Lewis Miller, a renowned floral designer, didn't just create beautiful arrangements—he created an *experience*. His spontaneous "Flower Flash" installations in public spaces turned floristry into performance art. It wasn't just about flowers; it was about branding, storytelling, and creating a viral marketing phenomenon. That's the kind of creative thinking that transforms a floral business into a movement.

The Bloom Mindset Shift: Here's How You Can Do It

If you're ready to stop struggling and start thriving, here's how you begin to shift your mindset today:

1. **Reframe Business as an Art Form**

Instead of seeing pricing, marketing, and strategy as boring or overwhelming, start seeing them as creative opportunities. Just like you design a bouquet with precision and care, you can design a business that supports your artistry.

Action Step: Write a short "Artist Statement" for your business. What do you want to be known for? What experience do you want your customers to have?

2. **Price Like an Artist, Not a Hobbyist**

Luxury fashion designers don't price their work based on fabric costs—they price based on value and experience. Michelin-star chefs price based on experience. Florists should do the same.

Action Step: Look at your pricing. Are you charging based on what feels "reasonable" or what your work is truly worth? Make one small pricing adjustment today that reflects your value. By increasing your prices, even just 5%, every penny goes directly to your bottom line—profit!

3. Embrace Marketing as Storytelling

Marketing isn't about "selling." It's about making people fall in love with your story, your brand, and your artistry. A flower shop is a stage, not just a store.

Action Step: Post one social media update today that shares *why* you do what you do, not just *what* you sell.

4. Automate or Delegate at Least One Task

You don't have to do everything yourself. Start small: automate appointment scheduling, outsource bookkeeping, or batch-create content for social media.

Action Step: Choose one task you hate doing and find a way to delegate or automate it this week.

Bonus Tip: Surround Yourself with Business-Minded Creatives

One of the biggest game-changers in my journey was connecting with mentors and fellow entrepreneurs who challenged me to think bigger. You don't have to figure this out alone.

Action Step: Find a business coach, join a mastermind group, or attend a floral business workshop.

Your Business Is Your Masterpiece

Floristry isn't just about flowers. It's about designing an entire *experience*, from branding to pricing to customer journey. The more you embrace the *art* of business, the more freedom, creativity, and success you'll have. You get to go from the "arranger" to the "architect" as you design your business structure.

> ❝
> A FLOWER SHOP WITHOUT A
> BUSINESS STRATEGY IS LIKE
> A BOUQUET WITHOUT WATER
> —IT WON'T LAST.
> ❞

Growth Hacks

Here are 10 lesser-known, insider hacks to help florists bridge the gap between artistry and entrepreneurship—some even a bit "gray hat," but all effective:

1. Psychological Pricing for Luxury Appeal

- **Strategy:** Instead of ending prices in .99 (e.g., $49.99), use whole numbers or .00 (e.g., $50 or $500). Luxury buyers associate rounded numbers with high-end, custom work.
- **Secret Trick:** Pricing at $97 or $197 instead of $100/200 can make products seem premium yet slightly more approachable.
- **Resource:** <u>Premium Pricing Strategies Explained</u> en.wikipedia.org+3en.wikipedia.org+3en.wikipedia.org+3

2. "Wedding Leak" Strategy for Instant Credibility

- **Strategy:** If you design flowers for a high-profile wedding, subtly "leak" behind-the-scenes prep shots (with permission or non-identifying features) to Instagram. Even hints of exclusivity boost perceived value.
- **Resource:** <u>How to Build a Hype Brand</u>ft.com

3. The "Emotional Upsell"

- **Strategy:** Instead of selling more flowers, sell an emotion. Example: "Would you like to add a 'first date memory' bloom to this bouquet?" Connecting an upsell to nostalgia increases conversion rates.
- **Resource:** The Psychology of Upselling

4. Silent Market Research via Instagram Polls

- **Strategy:** Before introducing new offerings, run an Instagram Story poll: "Which bouquet style feels more like *you*?" Customers feel involved, and you gather free market research.

5. SEO Manipulation Using Google Image Search

- **Strategy:** Rename your flower arrangement images with local search terms (e.g., "best-wedding-bouquet-LA.jpg"). Google Image search can drive surprising traffic to your website.
- **Resource:** Image SEO: Optimizing Images for Search Engines

6. Invisible Competitor Spying (The Smart Way)

- **Strategy:** Join local wedding Facebook groups *as a bride* (or a friend acting as one). Observe which florists get recommended and what customers really say about pricing.
- **Resource:** Competitive Analysis Using Social Media

7. "Scarcity Drop" Sales Trick

- **Strategy:** Announce limited-edition bouquets in small quantities (e.g., "Only 10 Peony Passion bouquets available this weekend!"). The perceived rarity increases demand.

8. Under-the-Radar Collabs with High-End Hotels

- **Strategy:** Approach boutique hotels and offer free lobby arrangements for one month. They get stunning décor; you get brand visibility + potential referrals from their event planners.
- **Resource:** How to Establish Strategic Partnerships

9. Automated "Client Surprise" Touchpoint

- **Strategy:** After a wedding, schedule an automatic email *six months later* saying, "Happy half-anniversary! Here's a discount for a surprise bouquet." This triggers repeat business effortlessly.

10. "Luxury VIP List" for Price Conditioning

- **Strategy:** Have an exclusive email list where subscribers see *your most expensive* arrangements first. This approach conditions them to expect high-end pricing before seeing lower-cost options.

Takeaway: Business mastery in floristry is an art. The right strategies—some creative, some psychological—can elevate your brand and profits beyond just floral design. Which of these are you excited to try?

Bloom Mindset Shift Transformation

Redefine Roles
Evolve and adapt

Embrace Entrepreneurial Mindset
Adopt business-oriented thinking

Make a Lasting Impact
Leave a significant legacy

Stay True to Artistic Vision
Maintain creative integrity

Sustain Creative Endeavors
Ensure long-term viability

Unlock New Avenues for Success
Explore diverse opportunities

What's Next...

In the next chapter, we'll dive into **branding as an art form**—how to create a signature style that makes your work instantly recognizable and turns customers into lifelong fans.

2

BRANDING AS AN ART FORM –
DESIGNING A BUSINESS THAT FEELS
LIKE A SIGNATURE BOUQUET

I n the last chapter, we shattered the myth that floristry is just about flowers and explored why mastering the *business* of floristry is just as creative as arranging blooms. Now, it's time to dive into one of the most powerful tools in your business arsenal: **branding**.

If you've ever looked at an arrangement and instantly known which florist created it, you've witnessed the magic of a strong brand. Your brand is more than just a logo or a color scheme—it's the emotional experience your clients associate with your work. And just like a perfectly balanced bouquet, a well-crafted brand has harmony, consistency, and an unmistakable personal touch.

Your Brand Should Be as Recognizable as a Signature Floral Arrangement

When you see a lush, romantic bouquet wrapped in burlap, you think Farmgirl Flowers. When you see dramatic, sculptural floral installations in a high-end hotel, you think Jeff Leatham. Their branding is so strong that their work is instantly recognizable, even without a logo or name attached.

Floral Branding Strategy

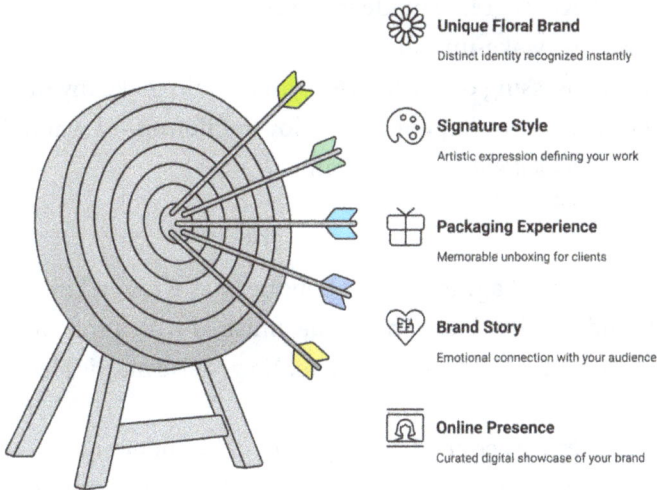

Unique Floral Brand
Distinct identity recognized instantly

Signature Style
Artistic expression defining your work

Packaging Experience
Memorable unboxing for clients

Brand Story
Emotional connection with your audience

Online Presence
Curated digital showcase of your brand

Now, let's ask an important question: **If someone saw one of your arrangements on a table at a dinner party, would they know it was yours?**

If not, don't worry. This chapter will show you how to create a floral brand as distinct as your artistic style. A brand that makes clients seek you out—not just for flowers, but for the unique experience you provide.

How I Built a Recognizable Floral Brand

When I started, I thought branding was just about having a pretty website and a nice logo. I quickly realized that branding is everything —it's the way you answer the phone, the way your bouquets are wrapped, and even the way your shop smells when a customer walks in.

But here's the truth: I didn't "get it" right away.

In the early days, I'd send out gorgeous arrangements... and then see clients repost them without tagging me. They loved the flowers, but they didn't *remember* who made them. That stung. One client even messaged me saying, "Hey, which florist did you use for this arrangement again?" I had made it myself.

That was my wake-up call.

I started obsessing over everything that could make my brand feel *like me*. I didn't just want people to enjoy the flowers—I wanted them to experience a *moment* with my brand.

So I invested in:

- **Luxury packaging** – Every bouquet was wrapped in branded cellophane and tissue, finished with a soft satin ribbon and a handwritten note. No generic plastic sleeves.

- **A signature scent** – I added a hint of lavender and eucalyptus to every delivery. To this day, clients say, "Your flowers smell like calm."

- **A cohesive color philosophy** – I leaned into a modern garden style with soft neutrals, creamy blushes, and one surprising "pop"—usually something moody like plum or coral.

- **A ritual** – Every arrangement came with a "care ritual" card. I wanted people to feel like they were tending to something sacred.

It took time, but slowly, people started tagging me without being asked. One bride told me, "I saw your bouquet on Pinterest three months ago. I *had* to find the florist behind it."

That's when I knew: I wasn't just selling flowers anymore. I was selling a feeling. And that's what branding really is.

Why Branding is the Difference Between Struggling and Scaling

Here's a scenario. Imagine two florists:

Florist A: The "Generic" Florist

- Offers a little bit of everything—classic, modern, boho, rustic.
- Uses stock photos on social media.
- Says "Yes" to any floral request, even if it doesn't match her style.
- Customers describe her work as "pretty," but they don't associate it with a unique brand.

Florist B: The Signature Brand Florist

- Has a distinct style that customers recognize instantly.
- Creates a signature packaging style that elevates the perceived value.
- Curates her social media feed with images that reflect her brand identity.
- Attracts customers who seek *her* specifically, not just flowers.

Which florist do you think is more successful? Branding isn't just about looking good—it's about becoming *memorable*.

Which branding strategy leads to more success?

Generic Branding
May attract a broader audience but lacks distinctiveness.

Signature Branding
Creates a memorable and unique brand identity, attracting specific customers.

Case Study: Farmgirl Flowers – The Power of a Signature Look
Farmgirl Flowers revolutionized the floral industry by doing one

simple thing: creating a *signature bouquet experience*. Instead of offering endless options, they created one beautifully curated daily bouquet wrapped in up-cycled burlap. This signature look became their calling card, allowing them to scale to a multi-million-dollar business.

The takeaway? **Branding makes you stand out. Branding makes you unforgettable.**

Case Study: Venus et Fleur – Turning Roses into a Luxury Experience

Venus et Fleur didn't just repackage roses—they redesigned the *desire* around them.

When founders Seema Bansal and Sunny Chadha couldn't find luxury flowers that matched their taste for elegance and longevity, they saw an opportunity: create eternity roses that lasted a year, wrapped in ultra-luxury presentation. But their real power move? Strategic brand partnerships.

Here's how they built their branding empire:

- **Influencer Alignment, Not Just Endorsement**
  - They didn't chase random Instagram influencers. They partnered with high-fashion, lifestyle, and beauty influencers who embodied *elevated taste*. Think: marble countertops, minimalist interiors, luxury unboxings. Every collaboration felt like it belonged in Vogue.

- **Exclusive Drops and Monogramming**
  - Venus created the allure of exclusivity by offering personalized monogram boxes—people weren't just buying roses, they were buying *status*. They even rolled out limited-edition collections with influencers that sold out fast, playing on scarcity psychology.

- **Visual Identity**

- Their brand visuals were carefully curated: cream and gold tones, crisp black boxes, and an editorial-style photo strategy. They didn't just *look* high-end—they controlled every detail like a luxury fashion house would.

- **Emotional Reframing**
  - Instead of promoting their flowers as a "gift," they promoted them as a *gesture of timeless love*. That subtle shift elevated the value perception—and allowed them to charge $400+ per box.

The Takeaway for Florists:

You don't need to be Venus et Fleur to use their playbook. Think about:

- Who you *partner* with (not just in followers, but in style).
- How your product presentation evokes exclusivity.
- What emotion your brand is really selling—beauty? sophistication? romance? nostalgia?

Branding isn't about reaching everyone. It's about becoming *unforgettable* to the right someone.

Building Your Signature Floral Brand

1. Define Your Signature Style

Your brand starts with your design style. What do you want to be known for? Romantic, wild garden-style arrangements? Sleek, architectural floral art? Bright, playful color palettes?

Action Step: Create a brand inspiration board. Use Pinterest or a physical vision board to collect images, color palettes, and packaging styles that resonate with your ideal brand identity.

2. Develop a Signature Packaging Experience

Luxury brands pay attention to packaging because it sets the tone for the entire experience. Whether it's a ribbon, a handwritten note, or custom wrapping, your packaging should make your brand feel high-end.

Action Step: Design a unique packaging element—this could be a wax-sealed envelope with care instructions, custom wrapping paper, or a signature flower added to every order.

3. Craft a Brand Story That Connects Emotionally

Your brand story isn't just *what* you sell, it's *why* you sell it. Customers connect with emotion, not products. What inspired you to start? What makes your work special?

Action Step: Write a short bio about your floral journey and infuse it with passion. Use it in your About page, social media, and marketing materials.

4. Curate Your Online Presence Like a Luxury Magazine

Your social media and website should be *curated*, not cluttered. Consistency is key—colors, fonts, and photography style should align with your brand identity.

Action Step: Audit your Instagram and website. Remove anything that doesn't align with your brand aesthetic. Replace stock photos with professional images of *your* work.

5. Set Boundaries with Your Brand

Not every client is the right fit. If you want to be known for luxury, you shouldn't take $20 grocery store-style bouquet requests. If you want to be known for bold colors, don't accept all-white wedding requests.

Action Step: Write a "Brand Manifesto" that defines what you say YES to and what you say NO to in your floral business.

Bonus Tip: Make Your Brand a Sensory Experience

Memorable brands engage the senses. Think of a high-end bakery— the smell of fresh pastries, the elegant packaging, the handwritten thank-you notes. Your floral business should *feel* like an experience.

Action Step: Identify three ways to engage the senses in your shop or packaging. Maybe it's a signature scent, a branded playlist, or a unique ribbon texture.

Branding is Your Business Identity

Branding isn't an afterthought—it's the foundation of a thriving floral business. A strong brand makes marketing easier, builds customer loyalty, and allows you to charge premium prices. When done right, your branding makes customers think, *I don't just want flowers, I want flowers from YOU.* "A well-branded florist doesn't compete on price—they compete on experience."

> **A WELL-BRANDED FLORIST DOESN'T COMPETE ON PRICE —THEY COMPETE ON EXPERIENCE.**

Growth Hacks:

1. "Signature Stem" Branding Trick

- Choose one unique flower or color that appears in every single arrangement you make. This makes your work instantly recognizable.
- Example: If you always include a sprig of rosemary or a single white ranunculus, customers will start to associate that detail with your brand.

2. "Luxury Brand Mimicry" Hack

- Study high-end fashion brands like Chanel or Hermès—how do they present their packaging, branding, and storytelling?
- Take inspiration from their color palettes, textures, or packaging techniques and apply them to your floral brand.

3. "VIP Unboxing" Social Media Boost

- Make your packaging so beautiful that customers *want* to film an unboxing and share it.
- Encourage this by including a hidden message inside the box or an Instagram-worthy ribbon technique.

4. "Invisible Logo" Technique

- Instead of placing a traditional logo on your packaging, use a consistent, recognizable color scheme, font, or design element that people associate with your brand without seeing your name.

5. "Signature Scent" for Brand Memory

- Infuse your shop, packaging, or bouquets with a subtle, signature scent (like a spritz of lavender water or a dab of a custom floral essential oil blend).
- Scent is one of the most powerful memory triggers—people will associate the smell with your brand.

6. "Micro-Influencer Packaging Collabs"

- Partner with a micro-influencer who aligns with your brand to co-design limited-edition floral packaging.
- This helps your brand reach their audience and creates exclusivity.

7. "Restricted Access" Luxury Trick

- Create an "exclusive" collection or service only available to certain clients (e.g., VIP clients get access to a secret floral menu or first dibs on seasonal arrangements).
- This builds brand desirability and makes people *want* to be in the inner circle.

8. "Brandable Language" Trick

- Invent a unique name for your signature bouquet style (e.g., "Parisian Romance," "Bohemian Luxe," "Timeless Garden").
- People don't just order "roses" from you; they order your *signature* style.

9. "Photographer Partnerships for Instant Credibility"

- Team up with wedding photographers who align with your aesthetic and provide free arrangements in exchange for professional brand-aligned images.
- This ensures your online presence always looks high-end without needing expensive branding shoots.

10. "Curated Color Palette Authority"

- Become known for a specific floral color palette or signature hues (e.g., "We specialize in pastel garden blooms").
- Customers will come to *you* for that look, rather than just shopping for generic flowers.

Takeaway: Branding isn't just about a logo—it's about creating an experience that people recognize, remember, and desire. These branding hacks will help florists craft a signature style that stands out in the industry. Which one will you try first?

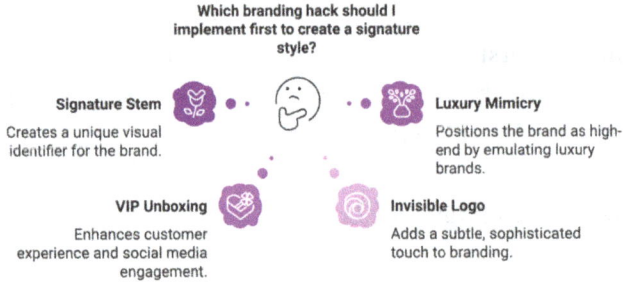

Which branding hack should I implement first to create a signature style?

Signature Stem
Creates a unique visual identifier for the brand.

Luxury Mimicry
Positions the brand as high-end by emulating luxury brands.

VIP Unboxing
Enhances customer experience and social media engagement.

Invisible Logo
Adds a subtle, sophisticated touch to branding.

What's Next...

In the next chapter, we'll tackle **pricing like a luxury designer**—how to stop selling stems and start selling experiences that customers are willing to pay premium prices for.

3

SETTING PRICES LIKE A HIGH-END DESIGNER: STOP MARKETING STEMS AND INSTEAD PROMOTE EXPERIENCES

W e explored the power of branding in the previous chapter, showing you how to make your floral business as iconic as a trademark bouquet. We now turn our attention to **pricing**, which frequently causes florists a lot of stress.

It's not only flowers you're selling. **Emotion, experience, and artistry are what you're selling.** *Furthermore, setting a fair price for your job is about worth rather than greed.*

This chapter will help you escape the undercharging trap, stop seeing prices in terms of flower stems, and begin viewing your work as an experience that clients are willing to pay for, much like high-end designers do.

The Psychology of Premium Pricing

Why would someone spend hundreds of dollars on a Chanel handbag when they could get a useful purse for fifty dollars? When they can find cheaper dining options elsewhere, why do they reserve seats at Michelin-starred restaurants?

It's about positioning, exclusivity, and experience, not just the goods. It's time for florists to adopt the same perspective that luxury brands do. **Consumers purchase more than simply flowers. They purchase the emotion those flowers evoke in them.**

Customers will believe your job is less valuable if you charge too little for it. Setting your prices carefully will draw customers who value floristry as an art form.

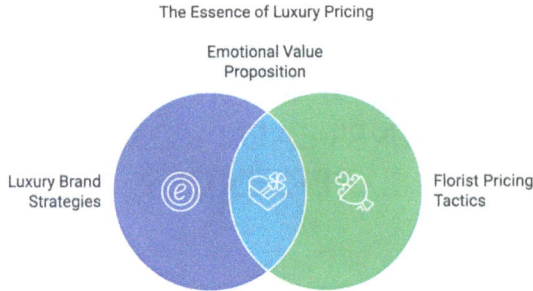

The Essence of Luxury Pricing

Emotional Value
Proposition

Luxury Brand   Florist Pricing
Strategies   Tactics

My Pricing Development: From Challenge to Strategy

In the beginning of my business, I set my prices according to what I believed customers would be willing to pay. "Okay, roses at cost are $1.50 a stem; I'll add a few bucks for labor, markup, and delivery," is how I would mentally calculate the price. Instead of pricing like a designer, I did it like a grocery store, stem by stem. The issue? I wasn't in charge of a supermarket. I was managing a creative company that needed emotional, time-based, and visionary work.

I initially believed that offering inexpensive prices would make me more "accessible." In reality, though, I became worn out and unappreciated. One morning at 2 a.m., I was designing $85 wedding centerpieces that ought to have cost $250. What about the customers? Because I had inadvertently positioned myself as the less costly option rather than the authority, they nitpicked, had second thoughts, and were expecting miracles.

Then after another significant occurrence, I reached my breaking point. After putting a lot of effort into the flowers and creating a beautiful arrangement, I discovered that my net profit was... $78.

That was it.

I investigated the pricing of luxury brands. I began to ask, "What is this experience truly worth?" instead of, "What can they afford?"

I changed my pricing from a cost sheet to a storytelling tool and called my bouquets "Romantic Runaway" instead of 24 rose stems.

"The Signature Ritual" for my weekly high-end customers.

Custom installs without line-by-line bills and with starting minimums

Everything changed when I began charging for the experience rather than the individual parts. I attracted clients who valued my vision. I made more money while working less hours. Above all, I rediscovered my passion for my business.

The Reasons Most Florists Have Trouble Setting Prices

Two categories of florists will be compared:

Florist A: The Under-appreciated Artist

- Lowers prices per stem in order to "remain competitive."
- Feels bad about raising prices and frequently gives discounts without being asked.
- Draws in cheap buyers who aren't impressed by the artistry.
- Puts in a lot of work simply to break even.

Florist B: The Luxury Floral Designer

- Knows her services are determined by more than simply the price of the flowers.
- Charges premium prices with assurance and provides quality and service to support them.
- Draws affluent customers who value exclusivity and artistry.
- Makes more money while putting in fewer hours.

Which florist are you interested in becoming?

Which florist category aligns with your business goals?

Underappreciated Artist
Focus on affordability and
volume

Luxury Floral Designer
Focus on premium pricing
and experience

Case Study: Jeff Leatham – The Power of Luxury Pricing
When people see Jeff Leatham's name, they don't think "florist."
They think *fashion for flowers*.

His achievement was a masterclass in positioning and premium
pricing, so it didn't happen by accident. Jeff began by constructing
surroundings rather than by detailing certain stems. His creations,
which can be seen anywhere from the Four Seasons Hotel in Paris to
celebrity weddings, resemble an art gallery composed of light and
petals.

This is his brand's pricing genius:

- **He made performance art out of floristry.**
  - The flowers appear as soon as Jeff enters a room.
  - He contributes to the brand experience by frequently
    being on location, rearranging flowers, adding drama,
    and giving clients the impression that they are a part of
    something unique.
  - That emotional investment? Premium rates are
    justified by it.
- **He included his *presence* in the cost.**
  - Customers pay for more than simply flowers. They are
    paying to *say* they hired Jeff Leatham. Like wearing
    Gucci or hiring a private chef, his name has come to
    represent prestige.

- **He doesn't explain pricing—he demonstrates it.**
  - Instead of using cost breakdowns to support his prices, his portfolio demonstrates why he is in high demand.
  - Every image conveys a tale of grandeur, opulence, and metamorphosis.
  - He allows the service's results to be the selling point.
- **His exclusivity is the selling point.**
  - Jeff Leatham is not someone you "shop."
  - You give him a commission. That one word changes the way customers view value.
  - He provides experiences rather than choices.

Takeaway: You must position yourself like a luxury designer if you want to charge like one:

- Be observed. Your value includes your visibility.
- Sell the transformation, not the transaction.
- Create experiences rather than just deliverables.
- The product includes confidence; therefore, let your brand speak for itself.

The goal of premium pricing is to elevate the narrative your work conveys, not to boost your ego.

Case Study: The Ritz-Carlton Floral Experience

The Ritz-Carlton and other upscale hotels have a whole department devoted to floral design. Their floral arrangements are an extension of the hotel's experience and brand, not just centerpieces. Guests are prepared to pay for perfection because they expect it. Working with luxury finances, Ritz-Carlton florists make sure that every little detail reflects the brand's exacting standards.

Takeaway: Your perceived worth increases when you associate yourself with upscale activities.

Here's How to Go About It: Changing Your Prices to Make More Money

1. Stop Charging by the Stem—Start Charging for the Experience

You are teaching your clients to view your work as a commodity when you break down prices into stems and labor. Instead, set your price according to the whole value you offer.

Action Step: Develop packaged prices for various client requirements, like as corporate installations, elegant event florals, and romantic bouquets. Show that it's worth more than just flowers.

2. Apply the Model of "Experience-Based Pricing"

Say something like, "This is a $150 floral experience designed to transform your space and create a lasting impression," rather than, "This arrangement is $150 because of these stems."

Action Step: Revise your pricing descriptions to emphasize storytelling, experience, and the feelings your florals evoke.

3. Use Tiered Pricing to Attract High-End Customers

Luxury brands offer different price points to give clients choices —why not do the same?

- **Entry-Level Experience:** More modestly arranged bouquets that are nonetheless representative of your company.
- **Mid-Tier:** Signature arrangements with premium flowers and personalized touches.
- **High-end luxury:** Personalized floral arrangements for affluent customers.

Action Step: Create a menu with tiers of prices so that clients may *choose* the experience they want.

4. Charge More for Your Signature Style

Customers should pay for your distinctive floral design if they desire it. You establish yourself as a sought-after authority when you create a signature design.

Action Step: Decide which element of your designs—a particular flower, style, or packaging—you can market as exclusively yours and charge more for.

5. Establish a Minimum Order Requirement

Why should you offer $20 arrangements when high-end designers don't? By establishing a minimum price for special orders, you may weed out bargain hunters and establish yourself as a high-end florist.

Action Step: Establish a minimum order value that guarantees profitability and clearly communicate it in your marketing.

6. Stand Firm on Your Prices

Pricing confidence is essential. Don't cut your prices right away if a client protests. Rather, describe the benefits they are receiving.

Action Step: Draft a script that will enable you to confidently address pricing arguments.

Bonus Tip: Create a "VIP Floral Membership" to Generate Repeat Business

Exclusion is key to the success of luxury companies. What if customers could sign up to regularly receive a luxurious floral experience?

Action Step: Create a membership program that allows customers to pay on a monthly basis for premium plans; this fosters repeat business and loyalty.

Pricing is Part of Your Brand

You convey the idea that your work is not worthwhile if you set your pricing too low. Strategic pricing draws in customers who value and respect your artistic abilities. With the correct pricing, your company can go from being a labor-intensive task to a *highly lucrative creative venture.*

> " LUXURY FLORISTS DON'T
> SELL FLOWERS. THEY SELL
> UNFORGETTABLE
> EXPERIENCES. "

Growth Hacks:

Florists can charge premium prices and draw in high-end customers by using these ten lesser-known pricing tricks and industry secrets:

1. "Anchor Pricing" to Make High Prices Feel Reasonable

- Even if no one purchases it, provide a high-end option (e.g., a $25,000 luxury wedding package). In contrast, it makes your mid-tier pricing appear more affordable.
- **Secret**: To make the other wines on the menu appear more reasonably priced, upscale restaurants put one outrageously expensive wine on the menu.

2. "Emotional Pricing" – Charge for the Moment, Not the Stems

- Don't charge "24 roses" for an anniversary arrangement. Price it as "The 'One More Year of Love' Arrangement".
- Clients are more willing to spend when they emotionally connect with the purchase.

3. "Luxury Tax Psychology" – Add a Premium Tier for No Reason

- Offer a 50% more costly ultra-premium option than your best-selling setup. To have the greatest, some customers *will* pay for it.

- For instance, placing a $300 luxury bouquet next to your $200 best-seller will encourage them to spend an additional $200.

4. "Branded Packaging = Higher Prices"

- Make an investment in **premium ribbon, wax seals, or personalized tissue paper.** Similar to designer handbags, exquisite packaging gives buyers the impression that they are purchasing a luxury good.
- **Secret:** Even if the blooms inside are identical, this increases perceived value and supports premium pricing.

5. "Event Floral Minimums = Profit Protection"

- Don't let events go below a certain threshold (weddings, for example, must cost at least $3,000). If you position yourself correctly, high-end clients **will not negotiate** because they expect a certain standard.
- **Secret:** Discreetly post this minimal price on your website so that only people who are prepared to pay will ask.

6. "The 'Bespoke' Trick" – Charge More for Customization

- Provide pre-set floral collections at a lower price, but charge an additional 20% to 30% for complete customization.
- Customers believe they are receiving VIP treatment, and you make the most money from customized orders.

7. Limited-Edition Bouquets: "Make It Exclusive"

- Introduce "limited edition" designs for specific seasons, which are more expensive since they are more scarce.

- **Secret:** People are more prepared to pay for an arrangement today if they believe it won't be accessible next month because scarcity forces them to act quickly.

8. "The Psychological Payment Shift" – Encourage Pre-Payment for Events

- To lock in cash flow early, provide a **discount for full prepayment,** even if it's only 3%.
- Because luxury clients are accustomed to paying in advance, you may avoid following up on payments later.

9. "VIP Subscription = Built-In Revenue"

- Provide a flower subscription service that allows high-end customers (such as upscale hotels, companies, or affluent people) to receive fresh bouquets every week or every month.
- **Secret:** Just like high-end fashion brands, this guarantees repeat business and fosters customer loyalty.

Takeaway: Perception, placement, and psychology all play a role in pricing. By using these exclusive tips, florists can **charge more confidently, draw in high-end customers, and make flowers a worthwhile experience.**

Which one are you most eager to put into practice?

Unveiling the Dimensions of Premium Floral Pricing

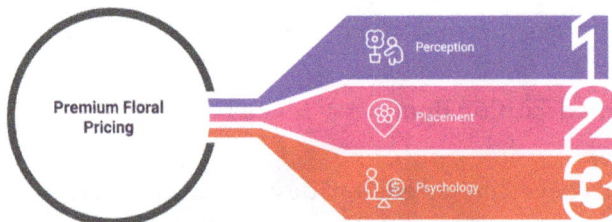

Premium Floral Pricing

Perception 1
Placement 2
Psychology 3

What's Next...

We'll discuss **creating a stress-free business model** in the upcoming chapter, which will cover how to scale your company sustainably while *working smarter*, not harder, and ultimately escaping burnout.

4

———

DESIGNING A STRESS-FREE BUSINESS MODEL – HOW TO STOP BEING OVERWORKED & UNDERPAID

I n the last chapter, we tackled the art of pricing and how to position your floral business like a luxury brand. Now, let's address the biggest problem many florists face: **being overworked and underpaid.**

If you've ever found yourself drowning in orders, running on fumes, and still wondering why your bank account doesn't reflect all your hard work—this chapter is for you.

The truth? The problem isn't just *pricing*—it's *structure*. Your business model determines whether you thrive or burn out.

In this chapter, you'll learn how to design a floral business that runs efficiently, maximizes profit, and—most importantly—gives you back your *time*.

Work Smarter, Not Harder

Most florists start their business thinking, "If I just take on *more* orders, I'll make more money."

Wrong.

More orders often mean: More stress. More hours. More exhaustion.

The key isn't to work *more*—it's to work *smarter*. Instead of filling every hour with labor-intensive work, let's build a **strategic** floral business model that works for you, not against you.

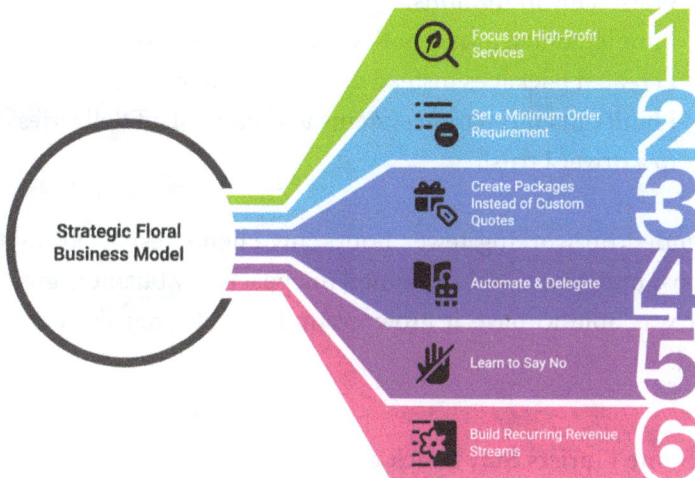

Unveiling the Strategic Floral Business Model

Strategic Floral Business Model

1. Focus on High-Profit Services
2. Set a Minimum Order Requirement
3. Create Packages Instead of Custom Quotes
4. Automate & Delegate
5. Learn to Say No
6. Build Recurring Revenue Streams

o

At one point in my career, I said "yes" to everything.

Evoery inquiry felt like an opportunity I couldn't pass up. Weddings on weekends, corporate events on weekdays, sympathy arrangements on my "days off," and last-minute Valentine's Day rush orders that had me arranging flowers past midnight. I wore my exhaustion like a badge of honor—proof that I was "doing the work."

But here's what I didn't see then: I was building a business that revolved around chaos, not sustainability. My phone never stopped buzzing. I couldn't go to dinner without checking my email. My back hurt constantly, and my creativity started to feel like a burden instead of a gift.

The breaking point came when I missed a close friend's baby shower because I had overcommitted to a triple-booked wedding weekend. I realized I was sacrificing the very life I was building a business to enjoy.

So I did the scariest thing: I paused. I took a hard look at my calendar, my pricing, and my systems—or lack thereof. And I made changes that felt terrifying at first but ultimately transformed everything.

- I raised my minimums.
- I implemented a "no" policy for last-minute jobs.
- I created packages instead of custom quotes.
- I built out automation systems and handed off deliveries to a driver I trust.

I ended up working fewer hours, my clients respected my time, and most importantly—I reclaimed my peace. My business grew, and then I was able to have it grow around my life, not the other way around.

Why Some Florists Stay Stuck & Others Scale

Let's look at two florists with the same talent level:

Florist A: The Burnout Florist

- Takes every order, regardless of size or profit margin.
- Works long nights doing everything herself.
- Struggles with cash flow despite being constantly busy.
- Feels exhausted, overwhelmed, and unmotivated.

Florist B: The Smart Floral CEO

- Focuses on *high-margin* services instead of high volume.
- Uses systems to streamline operations and free up time.
- Selects clients strategically and isn't afraid to say no.
- Runs a business that allows for creativity *and* freedom.

Which florist do you want to be?

Choose the florist type that aligns with your business goals and lifestyle.

Burnout Florist
Struggles with workload and profitability

Smart Floral CEO
Achieves balance and scalability

Case Study: How One Florist Scaled Without Burnout

Sarah, a florist based in New York, had talent pouring out of her fingertips—but her life? It was pure floral chaos. Every morning started with panicked texts. Every evening ended with spreadsheets, delivery mix-ups, or forgotten meals. She was booked solid and emotionally drained.

Her turning point came when a client emailed her at 2 a.m. asking to change the flower colors for their 9 a.m. wedding. Sarah hadn't slept, and she cried in her studio, wondering if this business was sustainable at all.

Instead of quitting, she restructured.

- First, she **raised her minimums** from $150 per event to $1,000. It felt bold, but it filtered out bargain hunters immediately.
- Next, she designed **three pre-set wedding packages** with defined deliverables and starting prices. She gave them romantic names like "The City Garden," which clients found easier to understand (and easier to say yes to).
- Finally, she **outsourced all deliveries** and trained a part-time admin assistant to handle quotes and invoices.

Within three months, Sarah had fewer clients but nearly doubled her income. She took her first weekend off in over a year and spent it wine tasting with her sister. She said, "I finally feel like a floral designer again, not just a floral factory."

Takeaway: Restructuring your business isn't about scaling back—it's about scaling intentionally.

Case Study: The Floral Studio That Mastered Work-Life Balance

Emma, a floral designer in Los Angeles, had a problem most creatives can relate to: she couldn't stop working.

Her phone was an extension of her hand. She'd answer DMs during dinner, respond to new client inquiries in bed, and accommodate every last-minute "Can you just..." request. Her clients loved her —but her friends barely saw her, and her mental health was suffering.

The shift started with a **single boundary**: no phone during meals. That one decision gave her the confidence to set more.

- She implemented **strict office hours**—no calls or emails after 6 p.m. or on Sundays. She communicated this clearly on her website and automated email responses. To her surprise, most clients respected it.
- She invested in a **client management system** that auto-replied to inquiries, shared her pricing guide, and scheduled consultations *without* her lifting a finger.
- She built a **production calendar** that blocked out weekends, ensured deliveries happened only two days per week, and gave her Mondays to focus on content and design.

The result? Emma didn't just get her weekends back—she got her *joy* back.

She now hosts flower-arranging workshops once a month, purely for creative fun. And she's booked months in advance, not because she says "yes" to everyone, but because she finally knows who her ideal client is—and how to serve them *without losing herself in the process.*

Takeaway: Boundaries aren't walls—they're the architecture of a sustainable business.

Designing a Business Model That Works for You

1. Focus on High-Profit Services

Not all floral services are created equal. Some drain your time with little profit, while others bring in high revenue with less work.

Action Step: Identify your most profitable services. This could be high-end weddings, corporate floral subscriptions, or large-scale installations. Focus on scaling *those*.

2. Set a Minimum Order Requirement

If you're spending hours fulfilling $50 orders, you're capping your earning potential. Set a minimum order price to attract higher-quality clients.

Action Step: Decide on a minimum order amount that ensures profitability—whether it's $500 for events or $100 for bouquets.

3. Create Packages Instead of Custom Quotes

Custom quotes take time, and clients often price shop. Packages make purchasing easier for clients *and* keep your pricing streamlined.

Action Step: Develop tiered packages for your services (e.g., "Luxury Wedding Package" or "Corporate Weekly Florals") to simplify booking.

4. Automate & Delegate to Free Up Your Time

Florists waste hours on admin work that could be automated or outsourced.

Action Step: Implement automation tools for invoicing, scheduling, and order tracking. Hire help for delivery, setup, or customer service.

5. Learn to Say No to Bad-Fit Clients

Not every client is the right client. If someone haggles on price, wants unrealistic deadlines, or doesn't fit your aesthetic—let them go.

Action Step: Write a clear "Who We Work With" statement on your website to attract ideal clients and repel time-wasters.

6. Build Recurring Revenue Streams

Fluctuating income is a florist's nightmare. A stable revenue stream—like floral subscriptions or corporate contracts—creates financial consistency.

Action Step: Offer a subscription service for weekly floral deliveries or corporate accounts with a fixed monthly fee.

Bonus Tip: Take Time Off Without Losing Money

A business that *only* runs when you're working is just another job. Design a model that allows for time off.

Action Step: Block out vacation days in advance and create systems so your business can run without you for short periods.

Your Business Should Work for You

A well-structured business model gives you *control* over your time, energy, and income. You don't have to be *busy* to be *successful*.

> " A SUCCESSFUL FLORAL BUSINESS ISN'T MEASURED BY HOW BUSY YOU ARE—IT'S MEASURED BY HOW PROFITABLE AND SUSTAINABLE IT IS. "

Growth Hacks:

Here are 10 little-known floral industry secrets and business model hacks to help florists stop being overworked and underpaid:

1. **"The Reverse Availability" Strategy – Control Your Calendar**

   - Instead of accepting every order that comes in, set **predetermined dates** when you're available for bookings (like luxury photographers do).
   - Clients book *you* when you're available, instead of you bending to their schedule.

2. **"Price Conditioning with Strategic Minimums"**

- List your highest-priced services **first** on your website and inquiries page.
- Example: If your top package is $5,000, customers who see it first will think your $2,500 option is "reasonable" instead of expensive.

3. "The 'Exclusive Club' Model for Recurring Revenue"

- Offer a **limited number of VIP floral subscriptions** for high-end clients.
- Example: "Only 10 spots available for our Luxe Home Floral Membership." This builds urgency and **locks in consistent income.**

4. "Automate 90% of Customer Inquiries"

- Create an **auto-response email** that answers FAQs, shares pricing, and **pre-filters clients** before they even speak to you.
- Example: "Click here to see if we're the right fit before booking a consultation."

5. "Profit-Per-Stem Formula" – Ditch Low-Margin Flowers

- Identify the **top 5 most profitable flowers** in your inventory and make them the **centerpiece** of your brand.
- Example: Some exotic florals **cost more but last longer,** which increases perceived value without increasing costs.

6. "Pre-Qualify Clients Without Lifting a Finger"

- Add an **application form** for high-end events instead of a basic contact form.
- Example: If they're not willing to **fill out a few details,** they likely aren't serious high-budget clients.

7. "Batch-Work Like a High-End Caterer"

- Instead of fulfilling random orders daily, set **specific design & delivery days** (e.g., all deliveries happen on Wednesdays & Saturdays; especially for those weekly subscription models).
- This **saves hours in setup and travel** while making your workflow predictable.

8. "Charge Extra for Rush Orders & Customizations"

- Offer **1-day or 2-day minimum order** windows, with a **rush fee** for last-minute requests.
- Clients who truly value your work will **pay extra for urgency.**

9. "Outsource Deliveries for Instant Time Freedom"

- Partner with **a local courier service or Uber-style floral delivery service** so you **never** have to personally deliver flowers again.
- **Time saved = more profitable floral design hours.**

10. "The 'Set It & Forget It' Content Strategy"

- Instead of **daily** social media posting, create **3 months of content in one day** and schedule it with tools like Later or Planoly.
- This keeps your brand **visible** without sucking up time.

Takeaway: A **stress-free floral business** isn't about working harder—it's about **setting boundaries, automating, and focusing on high-value clients.** Which of these are you excited to implement?

Stress-Free Floral Business

Boundaries
Set limits to prevent overwork

Automation
Streamline processes to save time

High-Value Clients
Focus on profitable and manageable customers

Stress-Free Floral Business
The ultimate goal of balance and efficiency

What's Next...

In the next chapter, we'll uncover **The 5-Star Florist: How to Elevate Customer Experience & Create Raving Fans.**

5

THE 5-STAR FLORIST – ELEVATING CUSTOMER EXPERIENCE TO CREATE RAVING FANS

I n the last chapter, we learned how to design a stress-free business model that prioritizes profit and efficiency while freeing up time. Now, it's time to talk about something that can make or break your floral business: **customer experience.**

Here's a secret most florists overlook: Your flowers are only *part* of what customers are paying for. The real magic? **How you make them feel.**

A florist who delivers a stunning bouquet *and* an unforgettable experience will create loyal customers who return again and again— and who tell everyone they know about your business. In this chapter, you'll learn how to turn one-time buyers into lifetime clients and raving fans.

People Remember How You Made Them Feel

Maya Angelou said it best: *"People will forget what you said, people will forget what you did, but people will never forget how you made them feel."* This applies to floristry just as much as any luxury experience.

If a customer orders an arrangement and it's beautiful, they'll be satisfied. But if that same order is wrapped with care, arrives with a handwritten note, and is presented in a way that makes them feel *special*, they'll be *delighted*.

Florists who focus on **elevating the customer experience** stand out in a crowded market and charge premium prices with ease.

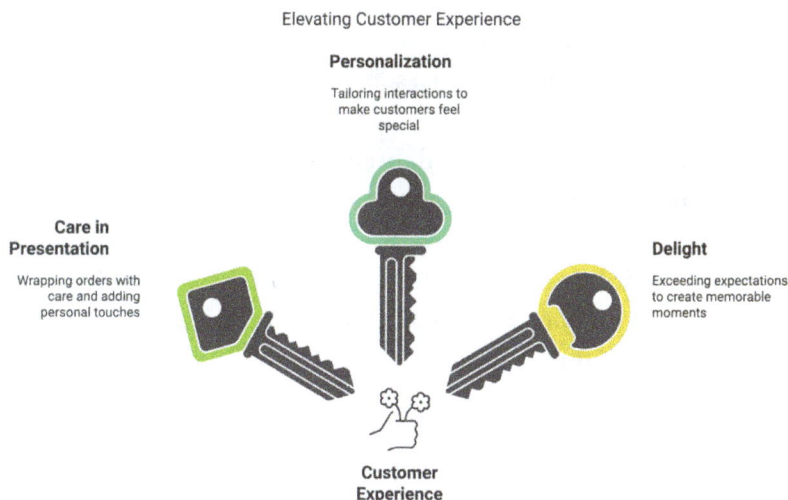

Elevating Customer Experience

Personalization

Tailoring interactions to
make customers feel
special

**Care in
Presentation**

Wrapping orders with
care and adding
personal touches

Delight

Exceeding expectations
to create memorable
moments

Customer
Experience

How I Transformed My Customer Experience

For a long time, I treated customer service like a checklist:

✔ Take the order

✔ Make the arrangement

✔ Deliver on time

And for a while, I thought that was enough. The flowers were beautiful, I was reliable, and customers seemed satisfied. But "satisfied" doesn't build a brand. "Satisfied" doesn't create loyalty. And "satisfied" definitely doesn't inspire someone to tell five friends about you.

I started noticing something: my competitors—some with *less* design skill—had waitlists. Their clients gushed about them online, tagged them constantly, and sent referrals without being asked. What were they doing that I wasn't?

Then it hit me: they weren't just delivering flowers—they were delivering *feeling*.

So I got intentional. I started treating every order like a small luxury experience:

- I added **a handwritten note** with each delivery— sometimes quoting poetry, sometimes just a warm message.
- I upgraded packaging with **branded wrapping and ribbon,** and added a signature sprig of rosemary—my "invisible logo."
- I began **following up** with clients a few days after delivery —not to sell, but to say thank you and make sure they loved everything.

Something magical happened.

Clients didn't just thank me. They raved. They sent voice messages. They ordered again—sometimes with tears in their eyes because they *felt* seen. That's when I realized: exceptional customer experience turns you from a florist into a forever memory.

Why Some Florists Struggle While Others Thrive

Let's compare two florists who create equally beautiful arrangements:

Florist A: The Average Transactional Florist

- Takes orders, fills them, and moves on.
- Doesn't build relationships with customers.
- Competes on price instead of experience.
- Has inconsistent customer retention.

Florist B: The 5-Star Experience Florist

- Adds personal touches that surprise and delight.
- Treats customers like VIPs, not just order numbers.
- Builds trust and emotional connections.
- Attracts repeat clients and premium pricing with ease.

Which florist do you think is building a thriving, high-end business?

Which florist model leads to a thriving business?

Average Florist
Focuses on transactions and discounts

5-Star Florist
Prioritizes customer experience and personalization

Case Study: How Melissa Built a 6-Figure Business on Experience

Melissa, a Chicago-based florist, had everything going for her—talent, training, even a storefront—but her sales were inconsistent. Some months were amazing; others left her scrambling to make rent. She tried discounts, social media ads, even flash sales. Nothing stuck.

Then she flipped the script.

Instead of lowering prices, she elevated her *customer experience.*

- She introduced a loyalty program that rewarded repeat customers with surprise upgrades—like a free mini arrangement on their fifth order.
- She redesigned her delivery presentation with luxury-inspired packaging: matte black boxes, gold-foiled stickers, and elegant branded wrapping.
- She created a VIP client list and invited them to early-bird holiday specials, exclusive floral drops, and even in-store "sip & stem" events.

Within a year:

- Her repeat customer rate doubled.
- She raised prices by 30%—and no one blinked.
- A single VIP client ordered 11 times in six months and sent four new customers her way.

Melissa didn't become more creative. She became more *thoughtful*. And that shift built her six-figure brand.

Case Study: Daniel's White-Glove Experience = Premium Clients on Repeat

Daniel, a luxury floral designer in Miami, didn't want to serve the masses—he wanted to serve *fewer clients at a much higher level*.

He crafted his entire business model around *white-glove service*.

- He offered a **private concierge number** for his top-tier clients—so they could text custom order requests without going through forms or websites.
- He hosted **exclusive floral experiences**: small, invite-only events at rooftop lounges where clients learned how to create arrangements with champagne in hand.
- Every order over $500 came with a **custom thank-you note**, hand-signed, and a special "gift bloom" tucked into the arrangement.

The result?

Daniel built a *waitlist*—not just for weddings, but for simple weekly arrangements. His average order size doubled in less than a year, and high-end clients didn't just return—they raved. One even said, "I wouldn't dare order flowers from anyone else. It's like cheating on my florist."

Takeaway: People don't fall in love with flowers. They fall in love with how you make them *feel* while receiving them.

Elevating Your Customer Experience

1. Make Every Order Feel Like a Luxury Purchase

High-end brands focus on packaging and presentation. Whether it's a single stem or a grand arrangement, the *unboxing experience* should feel special.

Action Step: Invest in premium wrapping, branded tissue paper, and a signature scent to make your deliveries feel exclusive.

2. Personalize Every Interaction

Small personal touches go a long way. Handwritten notes, remembering past orders, and using customers' names make a big impact.

Action Step: Start a client database where you track preferences and special dates (birthdays, anniversaries) so you can send thoughtful reminders.

3. Follow Up & Show You Care

Most florists forget about customers after the sale. A simple follow-up can turn a one-time buyer into a lifelong client.

Action Step: Send a "Thank You" email or message a few days after delivery, asking how they liked their flowers.

4. Create a "Surprise & Delight" Strategy

Unexpected gifts, exclusive perks, or a free upgrade can turn an average customer into a raving fan.

Action Step: Choose a small, affordable way to surprise customers—maybe a bonus bloom, a discount on their next purchase, or a free floral care guide.

5. Build a VIP Customer List

Make your best customers feel *exclusive* by giving them first access to limited designs, early holiday specials, or members-only workshops.

Action Step: Start a VIP email list and offer perks like priority ordering or seasonal floral subscriptions.

6. Create Instagrammable Moments

Your floral work should be so beautiful that customers *want* to share it. Branded packaging, custom ribbons, and stylish wrapping all contribute to share-worthy orders.

Action Step: Encourage customers to tag your business when they post your work and feature their photos on your social media.

7. Offer White-Glove Service to Premium Clients

High-end clients expect **convenience and exclusivity.** Offering VIP services elevates their experience and justifies premium pricing.

Action Step: Develop a concierge service for high-end clients—this could be priority ordering, same-day delivery, or personal floral styling.

Bonus Tip: Train Your Team to Deliver Exceptional Service

If you have employees, make sure they represent your brand with the same level of care you do.

Action Step: Create a customer service script for handling orders, responding to complaints, and adding personal touches.

> LUXURY ISN'T JUST IN THE PRODUCT—IT'S IN THE EXPERIENCE

Customer Experience is Your Competitive Edge

Florists who prioritize experience over transactions build **stronger brands, charge higher prices, and create lifelong fans.** The more memorable you make the ordering process, the more people will come back—and bring their friends.

The Experience-Driven Florist

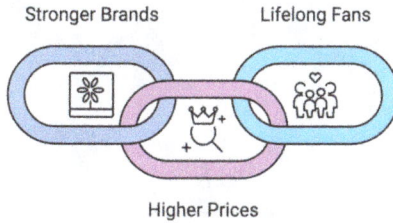

Stronger Brands   Lifelong Fans

Higher Prices

What's Next...

In the next chapter, we'll dive into **Marketing Magic: How to Sell Without Feeling Sleazy.** Get ready to learn how to attract dream clients without chasing them!

6

MAGIC OF MARKETING—SELLING WITHOUT HAVING A SLEAZY FEEL

L et's address **marketing**, a topic that many florists dread. You're not the only one who feels like a pushy salesperson when you hear the word marketing. Many creative entrepreneurs find it difficult to market themselves because they think that salespeople are shady or unauthentic. The truth is, however, that *marketing is about assisting others in discovering the beauty you provide, not about making sales.*

To draw in the correct customers without feeling like you're hunting them down, we'll explain in this chapter how to market your floral business in a way that seems organic, genuine, and successful.

Selling is Storytelling

Have you ever been utterly charmed with a brand because their story spoke to you rather than because they tried to sell you something? That's what storytelling-based marketing is all about.

Top florists, luxury brands, and upscale designers compete on connections rather than pricing. Consumers make purchases from companies they have a connection with, trust, and are inspired by.

Your objective? **Make your marketing more about stories, feelings, and the special experience you offer than just flowers.**

The Power of Storytelling in Marketing

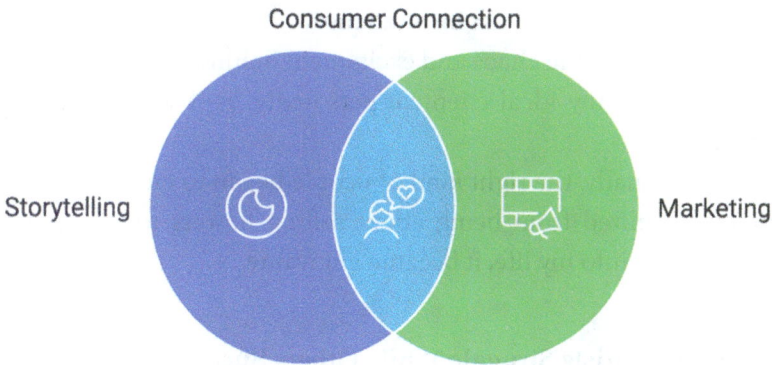

Consumer Connection

Storytelling   Marketing

My Story of Discovering My Passion for Marketing

When I was a new business owner, I saw marketing as an essential evil. I hated to write any kind of copy. I hired writers for my advertising, but they didn't seem to do well, so I started to doubt everything I did. And let's not even discuss the role that the internet played, as when I started, it was brand new.

Selling felt icky to me, and marketing meant selling. It raised concerns about coming across as conceited, annoying others, or appearing desperate.

So I said nothing.

I hoped that word-of-mouth would "just find me." Silence, however, is not a tactic. Even though my work was stunning, it wasn't consistently drawing in customers.

After a while, I began to notice new magazine ads. They shared a story. I always liked this florist's advertisements:

The message was heartfelt

The design was beautifully lit.

Using a straightforward call to action

It wasn't pushy. It lacked polish. It was honest. And I was hooked.

The realization that marketing isn't about selling came at that moment. Sharing is the key.

I began to show up as an artist with a story, not as a salesperson.

I wrote copy about what inspired me.

I was a part of the chaos and excitement behind the scenes.

I addressed my ideal clientele personally, as if we were already acquainted.

And gradually, the right kind of people began to emerge. Because marketing shifted from being about selling flowers to being about letting people into my life, it became enjoyable.

Why Some Florists Struggle While Others Succeed

Let's compare two florists with the same level of talent:

Florist A: The Silent Florist

- They post only when they remember.
- Nothing personal, just the final designs are shared.
- They have trouble bringing in new customers and rely on word-of-mouth.
- It seems that to compete, they must cut their pricing.

Florist B: The Magnetic Florist

- Regularly appears with interesting stuff.
- Shares personal views and behind-the-scenes stories.
- Draws in ideal customers who are emotionally invested in their work.
- Charges high costs because they aim to attract customers.

In your opinion, which florist is creating a strong brand?

Which florist's approach builds a stronger brand?

Florist A
Focuses on price
competition

VS

Florist B
Focuses on emotional
connection

Case Study: The Story of How a Single Florist Went Viral on Instagram

San Francisco-based florist Jessica was having trouble making an impression in a crowded market. She felt unnoticed on the internet, despite the fact that her creations were gorgeous—garden-style flowers with a wild, romantic edge.

Initially, still images of finished designs dominated her Instagram feed. Yes, it is pretty. Remarkable? No. The level of engagement was low. Reservations were irregular. She also began to question whether using social media was really worth the effort.

Then she started sharing instead of just posting.

- She shared time-lapse footage of herself in real time, complete with unkempt hair and bad lighting, assembling bouquets.
- She described her journey into floristry, including the burnout she endured at her previous 9–5 job, in sensitive captions.
- In order to motivate followers with color schemes, she started providing weekly "Floral Mood Mondays," small lessons, and flower care advice.

What took place?

In addition to her flowers, her fans thought they knew her.

Messages like *"I've been waiting to book you for my wedding for months!"* flooded her direct messages.

She gave up pursuing customers. Rather, customers contacted her and said, *"It had to be you."*

Jessica became more genuine rather than more polished. She became more magnetic as a result.

Case Study: The Wedding Florist Who Tripled Her Bookings

Austin wedding florist Megan has the talent, the flair, and the enthusiasm, but not the inquiries. She had no idea how to get in front of new clients and relied heavily on referrals. She felt stuck whenever she considered marketing. Where should I begin? What should I say?

Megan decided to market intentionally rather than attempting to be everywhere at once.

- On her website, she started a wedding blog where she published true love stories about the arrangements she made. In addition to vendor shoutouts and poignant narrative, each piece built connections and SEO at the same time.
- She collaborated with photographers who mirrored her style, delivering themed photo shoots in return for superior shots that improved the visuals of her company.
- She promoted her unique "Hill Country Romance" floral style in a targeted Instagram ad campaign that was directed at weddings and grooms within 50 miles of Austin rather than the general public.

The result?

In a single year, she increased her bookings. She implemented a 40% increase in her minimum package pricing. Even clients who responded, *"We already know we want you—we just need to confirm the date,"* began contacting her.

The secret wasn't doing *more* marketing.

It was using the right marketing—for the right people, with the right message.

Promotion That Seems Natural

1. Authentically Tell Your Brand's Story

Your audience is curious about your passion for floristry, your sources of inspiration, and what makes your work unique.

Action Step: Compose a brief account of your flower adventure and post it on your website, social media accounts, and promotional materials

2. Show Behind-the-Scenes Content

People enjoy seeing the creation process. Behind-the-scenes looks give your work a more intimate and significant vibe.

Action Step: Share a "day in the life" or time-lapse video of you making an arrangement for your company.

3. Share Testimonials & Client Stories

Prospective customers have faith in the experiences of others. Authentic consumer testimonials increase excitement and believability.

Action Step: Post pictures of their floral arrangement along with a brief testimonial from previous customers.

4. Maintain Consistency by Using Content Pillars

Are you struggling to decide what to post? Limit your content to three to five pillars, which are recurrent themes that facilitate marketing.

Examples:

- **Floral Advice & Education** (How to prolong the life of flowers)
- **Behind-the-Scenes** (Your Creative Process)
- **Personal Narratives** (Your Journey as a Florist)
- **Client Features:** Highlighting your previous work
- **Motivational Sayings and Mood Boards**

Action Step: List your content pillars and organize your posts according to them

5. Use Instagram & Pinterest to Your Advantage

For florists, visual media such as Instagram and Pinterest are a treasure trove. Every day, customers look for floral inspiration, so make sure your work can be found.

Action Step: To draw in local customers, post at least three times a week using pertinent geotags and hashtags.

6. Email Marketing: The Undiscovered Power of Sales

The majority of florists only use social media, yet genuine client relationships are developed through email marketing.

Action Step: Create your email list and send out a basic newsletter every month that includes exclusive deals, future specials, and behind-the-scenes information.

7. Execute Strategic Marketing (Without Trying to Sell)

Overuse of discounts can harm your brand. Rather, provide **time-limited experiences** that enhance your work without making it less valuable.

Examples:

- **Holiday pre-sales** (VIP access to seasonal arrangements)
- **Subscriptions for Flash Floral** (3-month limited subscription deals)
- **Workshops for exclusive clients** (teaching flower design)

Action Step: Arrange for a single, well-thought-out promotion for the upcoming season.

> THE GOAL OF MARKETING IS TO ATTRACT THE RIGHT CUSTOMERS TO YOUR COMPANY, NOT TO INCREASE SALES.

Connection is Key to Marketing

Dream clientele come easily to florists that use storytelling and regular content production. Simply show up, share your enthusiasm, and bring people into your world; you don't need to be an expert in sales.

Cycle of Storytelling and Content Production

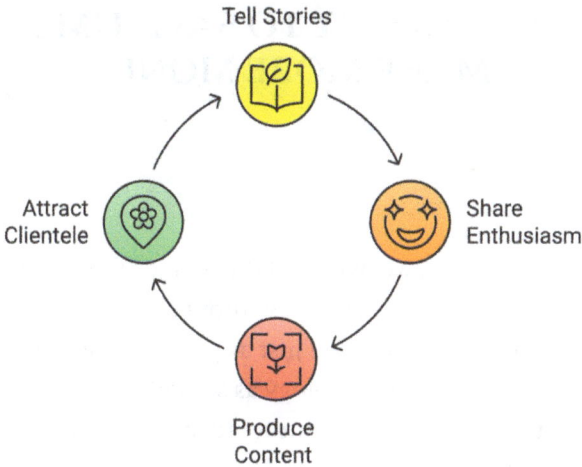

Tell Stories

Attract Clientele

Share Enthusiasm

Produce Content

What's Next...

The AI Florist: How to Use Technology to Save Time & Make More Money will be covered in the upcoming chapter. Prepare to learn how automation can help you expand your company without putting in more effort!

7

THE AI FLORIST—HOW TO USE TECHNOLOGY TO SAVE TIME & MAKE MORE MONEY

In the last chapter, we explored the magic of marketing and how to sell in your floral business without feeling sleazy. Now, we're shifting gears to something just as powerful: **technology.**

Many florists think of technology as something for big businesses, but the reality is that **AI and automation can help florists work smarter, not harder.** The right tools can save you time, streamline your business, and even boost your profits—without losing the personal touch that makes your brand special.

In this chapter, we'll uncover how AI and automation can help with everything from pricing and scheduling to marketing and customer service, so you can **spend less time on admin work and more time designing beautiful florals.**

Let Tech Do the Heavy Lifting

Imagine waking up to a fully scheduled day with pre-priced orders, automated customer follow-ups, and a marketing campaign running in the background—*all without you lifting a finger.*

That's the power of AI and automation. The best part? You don't need to be a tech wizard to implement these tools. Even small changes can make a *huge* difference in your daily workflow.

Florists who embrace technology:

- Save hours on administrative tasks.
- Reduce errors and missed orders.
- Create seamless customer experiences.
- Free up time to focus on creativity and growth.

Let's break down exactly how you can use AI and automation to transform your floral business.

Transforming Floral Business with AI

Time Savings	Error Reduction	Customer Experience	Creativity and Growth
Reduces administrative tasks	Minimizes mistakes in orders	Enhances customer interactions	Allows focus on innovation

How I Used Automation to Scale My Business

There was a time when I felt like I was running in every direction at once.

I was managing client emails, pricing every order manually, updating spreadsheets, and trying to keep my social media alive—while still designing, delivering, and running the day-to-day at my storefront. It was chaos. Creative, colorful chaos... but chaos none-theless.

At the time, tools like AI-powered chatbots weren't even an option or integrated into small business platforms the way they are now. But if they had been? I would've used them in a heartbeat.

What I *did* start doing was incorporating simple tech solutions that gave me my time back:

- **Automated invoicing** and payment reminders so I wasn't constantly chasing money.
- **Social media scheduling tools** to keep my online presence consistent, even when I was buried in events.
- **Pricing software** that helped me stop second-guessing my quotes and start charging confidently.

With each small upgrade, I felt a little less overwhelmed—and a lot more in control. Technology didn't take away from the personal touch of my brand. It protected it.

Now, with even more powerful tools available—like AI forecasting, chatbots, and automated CRM systems—florists today have an opportunity to grow in a way that's smarter, smoother, and more sustainable.

Why Some Florists Struggle While Others Scale Effortlessly

Let's compare two florists who have the same skill level:

Florist A: The Overwhelmed Business Owner

- Spends hours manually responding to customer inquiries.
- Calculates pricing on the spot, sometimes undercharging.
- Posts on social media randomly, when they remember.
- Feels burnt out trying to "do it all."

Florist B: The AI-Enhanced Floral CEO

- Uses AI-powered chatbots to handle basic customer inquiries 24/7.
- Has automated pricing software that ensures profitability.
- Schedules social media content in advance, staying consistent.
- Works fewer hours while making more money.

Which florist do you want to be?

Choose the florist type that aligns with your business goals.

Overwhelmed Florist
Struggles with time
management and scaling

AI-Enhanced Florist
Achieves efficiency and
growth

Case Study: How Rebecca Cut Admin Time by 60% Using AI

Rebecca, a wedding florist in London, was living the creative dream—on the outside. But behind the scenes, she was drowning. Her inbox was full of unread emails. Her quotes were delayed. And she was manually updating her website availability every. single. week.

Her turning point came after she double-booked herself for a wedding weekend... and had to refund a panicked bride.

That moment pushed her to explore automation—not because she loved tech, but because she couldn't afford *not* to.

- She installed a **chatbot** on her website that instantly answered the top 10 questions clients asked—like availability, delivery zones, and starting prices.
- She connected **invoicing software** (HoneyBook) that automatically sent quotes, contracts, and payment reminders—without her chasing a thing.

- She used **Later** to batch-schedule 30 days of content, freeing her up to focus on weddings, not her phone.

Within a few months, Rebecca had:

- Cut her admin hours from 25 to 10 per week.
- Reduced late payments to *zero*.
- Gained back her weekends—without sacrificing income.

Her clients didn't even notice the automation—they just saw a florist who was polished, responsive, and professional.

Case Study: The AI-Driven Floral Studio That Increased Profits

David runs a boutique floral studio in Toronto that serves luxury hotels and corporate clients. His installations are breathtaking, but behind the beauty was a logistical nightmare. Seasonal overstock. Missed invoices. Client follow-ups falling through the cracks.

David knew that to grow, he had to stop flying by the seat of his (beautifully branded) pants.

So he made some bold moves:

- He implemented an **AI forecasting tool** that analyzed past sales, seasonality, and client patterns to recommend *exactly* how much stock to order. The result? Less waste, more profit.
- He set up **automated subscription billing** for his corporate accounts, creating predictable monthly income without manual invoicing.
- He invested in a **CRM system** that sent out automated thank-you notes, reorder prompts, and seasonal offers to past clients.

In less than a year:

- His waste dropped by 40%.

- His revenue grew by 35%—without adding a single new client.
- He hired a junior designer—not because he was drowning, but because he had the time and systems to scale.

David didn't become more high-tech—he became more *intentional*. And his clients? They just saw a flawless floral experience and kept coming back.

AI & Automation Tools for Florists

1. AI-Powered Chatbots for Instant Customer Service

Customers expect fast responses, but you can't be available 24/7. AI chatbots can handle inquiries like:

- Availability & pricing inquiries
- Delivery status updates
- Common FAQs (e.g., flower care tips)

Action Step: Try chatbot tools like **ManyChat** or **Tidio** to automate customer conversations on your website and social media.

2. Automated Pricing & Quoting Tools

Stop second-guessing your prices. AI-powered pricing calculators factor in flower costs, labor, and market demand to ensure profitability.

Action Step: Use software like **Trellis**, **True Client Pro**, or **Details Flowers Software** to automate pricing for floral arrangements and event quotes.

3. Social Media Scheduling & AI-Generated Content

Instead of posting randomly, schedule your content in advance. AI can even help generate captions and suggest trending hashtags.

Action Step: Use **Later, Planoly,** or **Smart Business Toolbox** to plan a month's worth of posts in one sitting.

4. Automated Email Marketing to Keep Clients Engaged

Email is a goldmine for florists—**but only if used correctly.** Automation can send personalized offers, reminders, and thank-you messages *without* extra work.

Action Step: Set up an automated email series using **Flodesk** or **Smart Business Toolbox** to nurture your client relationships.

5. AI-Driven Inventory Management

Running out of stock—or over-ordering—hurts your bottom line. AI-powered tools can predict demand and suggest optimized ordering.

Action Step: Implement inventory software like **Stemcounter** or **Floranext** to manage your floral supplies efficiently.

6. Automate Booking & Payment Processing

Eliminate back-and-forth scheduling by letting clients book consultations or orders online.

Action Step: Use **Smart Business Toolbox, Calendly** or **Acuity Scheduling** to allow clients to book floral consultations with automatic reminders.

7. AI-Enhanced Floral Design Assistance

Believe it or not, AI can even assist with floral design—offering color palette suggestions and arrangement ideas.

Action Step: Experiment with AI tools like **Canva's AI-powered design features** to visualize floral arrangements before creating them.

Bonus Tip: AI for Wedding & Event Planning

Planning large-scale events? AI-powered event management tools can help coordinate timelines, budgets, and logistics seamlessly.

Action Step: Try **AllSeated** or **HoneyBook** for wedding and event planning automation.

> THE BEST FLORISTS DON'T WORK HARDER—THEY WORK SMARTER.

AI Isn't Replacing Florists—It's Empowering Them

Technology doesn't take away creativity—it *amplifies* it. By automating repetitive tasks, you free up more time for artistry, strategy, and client relationships. The florists who embrace AI **now** will be the ones leading the industry **tomorrow**.

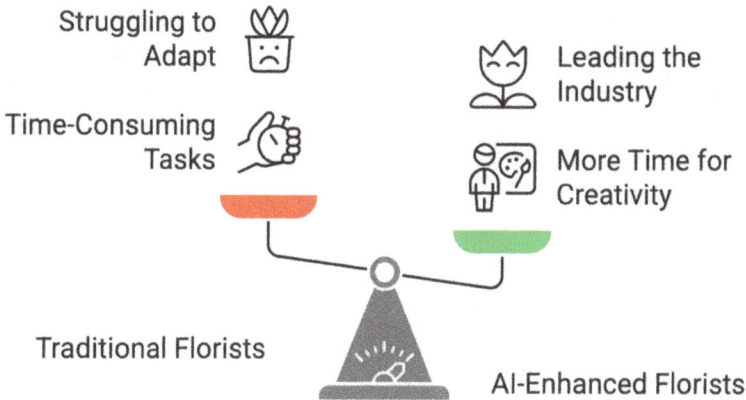

Struggling to Adapt

Time-Consuming Tasks

Leading the Industry

More Time for Creativity

Traditional Florists

AI-Enhanced Florists

Embrace AI for a flourishing future in floristry.

What's Next...

In the next chapter, we'll explore **Scaling Up: How to Move from**

Orders to Contracts. Get ready to learn how to secure high-end floral contracts that create long-term stability for your business!

8

SCALING UP – HOW TO SHIFT FROM ORDERS TO CONTRACTS

W e looked at how automation and artificial intelligence (AI) can help florists save time, improve productivity, and boost revenue in the last chapter. **Moving from one-time orders to high-value contracts will help you scale your business** and take it to the next level.

This chapter is for you if you've ever been caught up in a vicious cycle of erratic sales, persistently seeking out new clients, or battling seasonal slowdowns. Securing continuous, high-value contracts that provide steady revenue is more **important for long-term, sustainable success in the floral industry** than just selling more arrangements.

It will teach you how to move from one-time sales to recurring relationships with hotels, event planners, corporate clients, and subscription-based consumers in order to **scale your business without experiencing burnout and stabilize your revenue.**

Contracts Provide Stability & Profitability

Orders for one-off flowers are uncertain. While some months are excruciatingly sluggish, others could be flourishing. Contrarily, contracts offer **steady income, predictable labor, and financial security.**

Long-term contract florists:

- Maintain a consistent income flow, especially during weak seasons;
- Reduce marketing time because customers come back on their own;
- Develop closer bonds with high-end clients.
- Make more time for creative and business development.

Let's examine how to transition from selling individual orders to securing lucrative relationships that help your company grow.

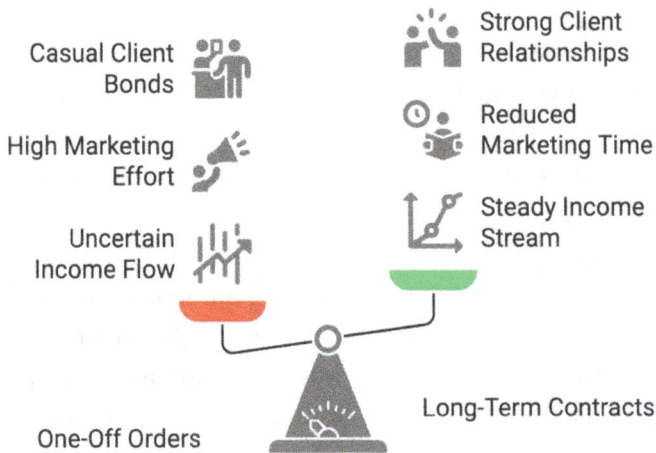

Casual Client Bonds

High Marketing Effort

Uncertain Income Flow

Strong Client Relationships

Reduced Marketing Time

Steady Income Stream

One-Off Orders

Long-Term Contracts

Contracts provide stability and growth.

How I Made the Switch from One-Time Purchases to Ongoing Agreements

I spent years trapped on the one-off order hamster wheel.

There were new questions, fresh suggestions, and additional

tension every week. I would prepare myself for the mayhem if a holiday was approaching. If not? I would hope that there would be enough orders to pay for the costs.

Marketing, following up, and lowering prices to seal a contract made me feel like I was constantly in sales mode. The lows caused concern, but the highs were high.

Then it dawned on me one afternoon as I was delivering an arrangement to a nearby legal practice: "**They always have flowers in here.**" Why don't I supply them each week myself?

Everything changed with that one simple remark.

I proposed to them a weekly flower subscription service that would be customized for their workspace. "Yes," they said.

A hotel client followed. Next, a spa. Next, a high-end restaurant.

I had steady money all of a sudden, even before I received any orders for weddings or holidays. I could make plans. I was able to breathe.

Most significantly, I could produce without having to worry about daily sales pressure.

The power of switching from orders to contracts is that. It alters not only your earnings but also how you interact with the business you represent.

Let's now discuss how you can follow suit.

Why Some Florists Scale While Others Stay Stuck

Let's compare two florists with the same skill level:

Florist A: The One-Time Order Hustler

- Depends on one-off purchases.
- Struggles with decreases in cash flow and slow seasons.
- Spends too much effort on marketing to attract new customers.
- Feels overpowered by erratic revenue all the time.

Florist B: The Contract-Based Floral CEO

- Has several sources of recurrent income.
- Enjoys predictable work and stable cash flow.
- Spends more time designing and less time marketing.
- Focuses on long-term client connections in order to work more efficiently.

Which florist are you interested in becoming?

Choose the best business model for long-term growth and stability.

One-Time Orders
Focus on immediate sales and individual transactions

VS

Contract-Based
Emphasize long-term relationships and recurring revenue

Case Study: How a Single Florist Used Contracts to Grow a Six-Figure Business

Like many florists, Samantha's company was centered around weddings, and she operated a boutique flower studio in Miami. Although the art was exquisite, the stress? Relentless.

Her income seemed to fluctuate between strong months and dry times. She was creatively exhausted from the continual pressure to fill her calendar, and she loathed the slow season.

She began to think differently at that point.

- She recognized **high-end real estate firms and office buildings** in her neighborhood—businesses that sought to dazzle customers with luxury surroundings.
- She produced two **floral subscription packages,** one basic and one upscale, complete with transparent pricing and images of previous designs.

- She **marketed them as brand boosters** that gave rooms a cozy, polished, and sophisticated atmosphere rather than as "flowers."

In a matter of months, she signed agreements with two spas and three legal companies.

- She started a seasonal décor service that generated steady income all year long.
- Her wedding income turned into bonus money rather than survival money.
- These days, her company is based on profitability and predictability. Because her contracts provide monthly income flow, she is no longer concerned about seasonal downturns.

Takeaway: Scaling is about creating more intelligent money streams that encourage your creativity, not about accepting more.

Case Study: Carlos' Business Was Revolutionized by the Hotel Partnership

Carlos was a New York-based floral artist renowned for his chic, contemporary style. Who were his most important customers? Occasionally, upscale hotels will buy flowers for private rooms and lobby displays.

He initially handled every order as a one-time task. However, he had to manage hundreds of small daily orders to survive, and he couldn't rely on hotels contacting him regularly, making it a constant struggle.

Then he understood that although his hotel patrons enjoyed his work, they detested having to place new orders. He therefore made it easy for them.

- He created a unique floral design for every hotel, considering seasonality, brand colors, and visitor demographics.

- Delivery, setup, breakdown, and weekly refreshes were all included in his white-glove service, which required no work on the part of the employees.
- Seasonal improvements, such as VIP guest suites or holiday lobby décor, were incorporated into his tiered contracts.

One hotel became three.

Three turned into five.

Soon after, he had a consistent flow of high-ticket, low-maintenance clients who gave him a recurring monthly revenue.

Although he now does it on his own terms, Carlos still continues to design weddings and other special events. His company is now characterized by stability, elegance, and high-level client relationships rather than hustling.

Takeaway: One-time customers will frequently become long-term partners if you treat them like such.

Getting High-Value Floral Contracts

1. Identify Your Best Contract Opportunities

Determine Your Greatest Contract Opportunities

Long-term contracts are not appropriate for every client. Typically, the greatest possibilities originate from:

- Corporate Offices: Fresh flowers in the lobby are a hit with law firms, tech companies, and real estate agents.
- Hotels & Resorts: Elegant floral arrangements are essential for upscale establishments' lobby areas and guest rooms.
- Restaurants and spas: Expensive establishments prefer a dependable atmosphere with vibrant flower touches.
- Event planners: These experts want a preferred florist because they plan numerous weddings and events each year.

Action Step: List ten local companies that might profit from continuing floral services.

2. Design a Unique Subscription Package for Flowers

Make a planned offer to clients regarding recurring services rather than waiting for them to inquire.

- Weekly or biweekly flower arrangements for workplaces, lodging facilities, or restaurants could be included in a floral subscription package.
- Services for holiday and seasonal décor (such as spring refreshes, Valentine's Day, and Christmas).
- First dibs on personalized floral arrangements for special occasions.

Action Step: To accommodate varying price ranges, provide a minimum of two package tiers (such as Standard & Luxury).

3. How to Approach Corporate Clients with a Strong Pitch

Until you demonstrate the value, businesses may not realize they need flowers.

When presenting to business clients:

- Highlight how flowers improve their brand image
- Emphasize stress-free convenience (automatic delivery, weekly fresh flowers)
- Offer personalized options that complement their corporate colors and decor.

Action Step: Write a polished email template outlining your subscription services for flowers and distribute it to your top ten prospective customers.

4. Establish Connections with Venues and Event Planners

- Your greatest source of recurring revenue may be venue and event coordinators. They will recommend you to every client they book if they are pleased with your service.

Action Step: Meet event coordinators and venues by going to regional wedding expos or networking gatherings.

5. Automate Your Contract Management

It can take a lot of time to manage several contracts. Streamline your workflow by automating client follow-ups, renewal reminders, and bills.

Action Step: Manage client contracts and billing with software such as HoneyBook or **QuickBooks**.

Contracts Give You Freedom

You can establish long-term client connections, dependable revenue, and financial security by switching from one-time orders to continuing contracts. You may concentrate on providing outstanding floral experiences rather than continuously seeking for new clients.

> **SUSTAINABLE SUCCESS IN FLORISTRY ISN'T ABOUT SELLING MORE—IT'S ABOUT SELLING SMARTER.**

Growth Hacks: Scaling from Orders to Contracts

Here are 9 growth strategy secrets and business model hacks to help florists get floral contracts.

The First 6 Growth Strategies to Get Floral Contracts

1. The Trojan Horse of the Trial Bouquet

Provide a complimentary "trial bouquet" that complements their branding to ideal clientele, such as boutique hotels, spas, or legal firms. A card with the words, "This is how your space could look— every week, stress-free," could be included. Next, make a proposal for your subscription package.

Why it works: Professionals with busy schedules seek answers, not shopping.

2. The Technique of Lobby Leverage

In return for branding placement, give one prominent location a discount. Share images on social media on a regular basis and include a brief tag such as "Floral design by [Your Business]."

Why it works: Particularly in the hospitality industry, a single visible install can generate over ten inquiries.

3. The Agreement for Event Insiders

Present a reference or retainer agreement that is ready to sign to planners, venues, and concierge services. When they include you in their packages, offer a commission, a discount, or other benefits.

Why it works: Make it easy for event planners to recommend you; they adore turnkey partners.

4. The Stem Lock-In Signature

Only long-term contracts will allow you to create a unique floral feature that becomes a part of the client's look, such as a signature bloom or branded wrap.

Why it works: They won't switch once your flowers are a part of their brand.

5. The Subscription for the Silent Setup

Offer a "No-Touch Floral Experience" that includes upkeep, seasonal designs that change, and predetermined delivery dates. Provide tiers of plans: Prestige, Signature, and Essentials.

Why it works: Busy, high-end clients find set-it-and-forget-it services attractive.

6. The Email Pitch-Perfect Drop

Send ten ideal clients a well-written, benefits-focused email that includes:

- Stunning images of your previous installations
- Bullet points on branding, ambience, and convenience
- A clear call to action: "Let's schedule a call to customize your plan."

Why it works: The pitch is never sent by most florists. Reaching out professionally equals immediate credibility.

3 Top Growth Strategies for Hotels and Expensive Dining Establishments

7. The Amplifier for the Guest Experience

Provide reserved tables or suites with VIP micro-arrangements that are intended to create Instagrammable opulence. Add branded elements and optional menus or fragrance combinations using QR codes.

Why it works: Turnkey, shareable beauty is a favorite of luxury venues. You become the designer of their visitor experience.

8. The Strategy of the Seasonal Showpiece

Make a pitch for a dramatic installation every three months, such as "Botanical Noir" or "Winter Bloomscape." Press-worthy displays should be included with a tiered design contract.

Why it works: Large installs generate a lot of attention and establish you as their preferred artist.

9. The Power Play of the Concierge

Make a flower menu that is exclusive to concierges for special events like birthdays, engagements, and surprises. Provide simple QR codes and establish billing for hotel charges.

Why it works: Your guests won't ever need to purchase elsewhere thanks to the concierge acting as your quiet sales force.

Pro Tip: To pitch exclusive venues, create a chic "Luxury Partner Deck" that includes testimonials, packages, and images, much like a fashion brand lookbook.

Cycle of Contract-Based Growth

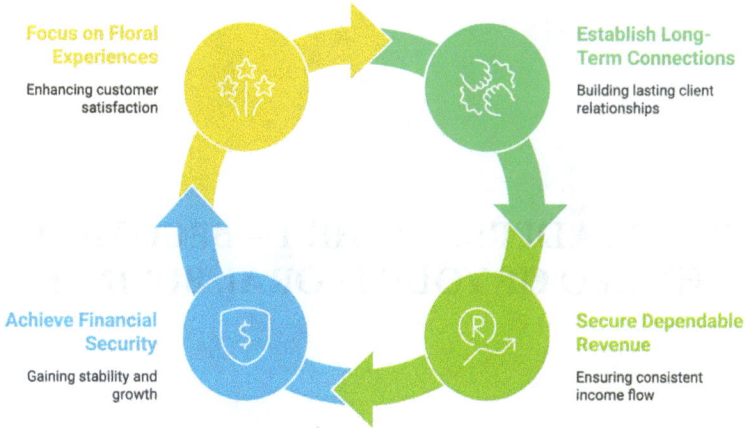

Focus on Floral Experiences
Enhancing customer satisfaction

Establish Long-Term Connections
Building lasting client relationships

Secure Dependable Revenue
Ensuring consistent income flow

Achieve Financial Security
Gaining stability and growth

What's Next...

In the next chapter, we'll dive into **The Leadership Shift—Becoming the CEO of Your Floral Business.** Get ready to step into your role as a confident business owner and visionary leader!

9

THE LEADERSHIP SHIFT – BECOMING THE CEO OF YOUR FLORAL BUSINESS

In the last chapter, we covered how to scale your floral business by shifting from one-time orders to lucrative contracts. Now that you have steady income streams and a strong client base, it's time for the biggest shift of all—**stepping fully into your role as a leader.**

Many florists start as solopreneurs, doing everything themselves. But to truly grow and create a sustainable, thriving business, you need to transition from **being a florist who works in the business** to **a CEO who runs the business.**

In this chapter, we'll explore how to develop a leadership mindset, build a reliable team, and implement systems that allow your business to grow without requiring your hands on every single bouquet.

Leadership Is a Mindset Shift

There's a difference between being a skilled florist and being a **floral business owner.** Many talented florists stay stuck because they never make the mindset shift from worker to leader. They believe no one can do things as well as they do, so they refuse to delegate—and as a result, they become the bottleneck in their own business.

Florists who embrace leadership:

- Free up time to focus on high-level business strategy.
- Build a strong team that supports business growth.
- Work *on* the business instead of being trapped *in* it.
- Avoid burnout and create a sustainable long-term career.

Let's break down exactly how to step into your leadership role and grow your business beyond yourself.

From Florist to CEO

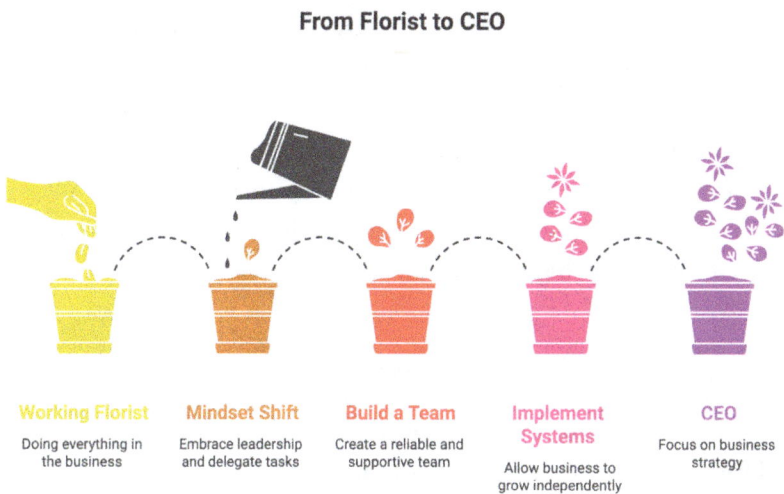

| **Working Florist** | **Mindset Shift** | **Build a Team** | **Implement Systems** | **CEO** |
| Doing everything in the business | Embrace leadership and delegate tasks | Create a reliable and supportive team | Allow business to grow independently | Focus on business strategy |

How I Transformed from Overworked Florist to Floral CEO

For years, I wore every hat in my business—and I wore them like badges of honor.

Designer. Deliverer. Accountant. Social media manager. Customer service rep. There were days I didn't eat a proper meal because I was too busy making sure every single detail was "just right."

At the time, I believed that doing it all myself was the only way to maintain quality. That no one could possibly care about my brand like I did. That "delegating" was something for big businesses, not floral studios like mine.

But eventually, the burnout crept in. I was tired, resentful, and stuck. I wasn't growing—I was just surviving.

The turning point came when I finally hired my first assistant. And you know what? She didn't just help—she *freed* me.

- I had time to actually think strategically.
- I created systems instead of reinventing the wheel every week.
- I trained her in my design philosophy so she could replicate my style—and she did it beautifully.

That was the moment I stopped being just a florist and stepped into the role of *CEO*. Not because I had a big team or a fancy office—but because I finally understood what leadership really meant: building something bigger than myself.

Why Some Florists Stay Stuck While Others Scale

Let's compare two florists who have the same level of talent:

Florist A: The Overworked Solo Florist

- Does everything alone because "no one else can do it right."
- Works long hours but never seems to get ahead.
- Struggles to take vacations or time off without the business suffering.
- Feels stuck at a certain income level because there's no room to grow.

Florist B: The Floral CEO

- Delegates tasks so they can focus on high-level strategy.
- Invests in training a team to ensure consistency.
- Has systems in place so the business runs smoothly without them.
- Enjoys work-life balance while growing revenue.

Which florist do you want to be?

Choose the best approach for business growth and personal well-being.

Overworked Solo Florist
Leads to burnout and stagnation

Floral CEO
Enables growth and balance

Case Study: How Amanda Built a Scalable Team

Amanda owned a floral studio in Las Vegas and had built a solid reputation for her lush, elegant event work. But behind the scenes, she was completely maxed out.

She was doing *everything*—consultations, ordering, flower prep, social media, admin, invoicing, delivery—and it was taking a toll on her health, creativity, and relationships. She couldn't take a full day off without feeling like the business would fall apart.

Her breakthrough came after a particularly grueling wedding season. She realized that if she didn't make a change, she was going to burn out—or worse, start resenting the business she once loved.

Here's what she did:

- Hired a **studio assistant** two days a week to handle cleaning buckets, processing flowers, and managing deliveries. It gave her hours back instantly.
- Outsourced **bookkeeping and invoicing** to a virtual assistant, which reduced errors and mental clutter.

- Created a **design style guide** for her arrangements, complete with color palettes, signature elements, and core mechanics, so that any new hire could be trained in her brand aesthetic.
- Developed a **"client journey" system** that mapped out every touchpoint from inquiry to post-event follow-up— allowing her assistant to confidently manage admin without constant check-ins.

The results?

- She doubled her revenue the following year.
- She gained the confidence to take weekends off.
- And most importantly—she *fell back in love* with her business.

Takeaway: Amanda didn't just grow her team—she grew her capacity to lead. And that changed everything.

Case Study 2: The Leadership Leap That Changed Nicholas' Business

Nicholas was an incredible designer based in Denver, known for dramatic floral installations and high-end editorial shoots. But as demand for his work grew, so did the pressure. He was turning down opportunities—not because he lacked talent, but because he lacked bandwidth.

He had one part-time assistant, but still insisted on handling every single bouquet, every consultation, every event setup himself. He told himself it was about "maintaining quality"—but deep down, he feared losing control.

The moment that changed everything?

He missed a family celebration because he was stuck assembling centerpieces—centerpieces he knew someone else could've done with the right training.

Nicholas finally decided to lead, not just labor.

- He brought on a **lead designer** and trained them over six weeks using mock installs and design reviews.
- He created a **workflow chart** for event execution—from prep to load-out—so everyone knew their role and the process ran like clockwork.
- He held **weekly team meetings** to review goals, upcoming events, and challenges—something he once thought was "too corporate," but soon found essential.

The transformation was massive:

- He scaled to serve double the number of events—without compromising quality.
- His clients felt more taken care of because communication improved.
- He had *space* again—space to dream, to grow, and to reconnect with his personal life.

Takeaway: Nicholas didn't lose control when he stepped into leadership—he finally *gained* it.

Building a Team & Leading with Confidence

1. Identify What You Should Stop Doing

The first step in stepping into leadership is **letting go** of tasks that don't require *your* expertise.

Action Step: Make a list of everything you do in your business. Highlight the tasks someone else could handle (e.g., deliveries, emails, invoicing, flower processing).

2. Hire & Train the Right People

Hiring can feel scary, but bringing on the right help is a game-changer. Start with part-time support and grow from there.

- Roles you might consider hiring for:
  - Studio assistant (prep & deliveries)
  - Administrative assistant (emails, invoicing, scheduling)
  - Event setup crew
  - Social media manager

Action Step: Write a job description for your first (or next) hire.

3. Build Opportunity & Performance Drivers Instead of SOPs

Instead of relying on lengthy, rigid SOPs, focus on building **Opportunity & Performance Drivers**—systems that drive predictable results while allowing for flexibility and innovation. Opportunity Drivers attract new clients consistently, while Performance Drivers ensure your team can deliver exceptional floral experiences without constant oversight.

Action Step: Identify the core activities that drive revenue (opportunity) and customer satisfaction (performance). Map out the key actions that fuel these drivers, such as automating lead generation, optimizing client onboarding, and streamlining event execution. Develop repeatable, scalable processes that allow your business to operate at a high level without micromanagement.

4. Set Boundaries & Protect Your Time

As a leader, your time should be spent on *big-picture growth*, not small daily tasks.

Action Step: Set office hours, block out creative time, and delegate routine tasks so you can focus on CEO-level decisions. Establish clear communication protocols to prevent unnecessary interruptions.

5. Develop a Leadership Mindset

Being a great leader means:

- Trusting your team to handle tasks.
- Making decisions based on strategy, not just emotions.
- Prioritizing the *long-term vision* over short-term busyness.
- Investing in continuous learning and personal development.

Steps to Leadership in Floral Business

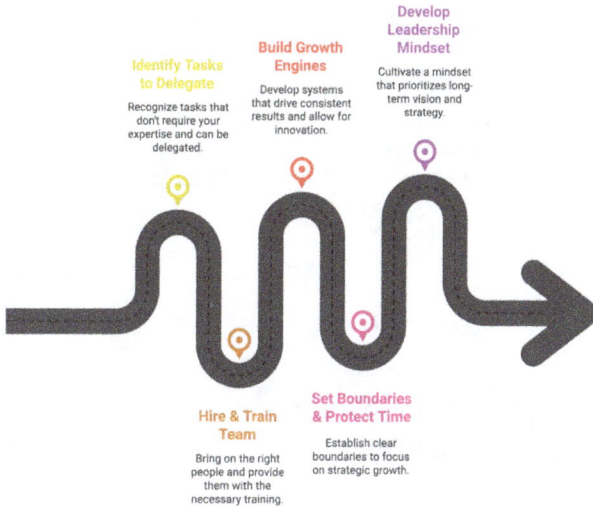

Develop
Leadership
Mindset

Cultivate a mindset
that prioritizes long-
term vision and
strategy.

Build Growth
Engines

Develop systems
that drive consistent
results and allow for
innovation.

Identify Tasks
to Delegate

Recognize tasks that
don't require your
expertise and can be
delegated.

Hire & Train
Team

Bring on the right
people and provide
them with the
necessary training.

Set Boundaries
& Protect Time

Establish clear
boundaries to focus
on strategic growth.

Action Step: Start treating yourself as the CEO of your business. Set quarterly goals, track progress, and focus on high-impact activities. Read books on leadership, attend business development seminars, and seek mentorship from successful entrepreneurs.

Bonus Tip: Learn to Say No & Stay in Your Zone of Genius

Many florists stay overworked because they take on *everything*, even jobs that don't align with their business goals.

Action Step: Set clear criteria for what types of projects and clients you take on, and say no to anything outside that focus. Establish premium pricing to attract high-value clients and filter out low-profit work.

Leadership Gives You Freedom

The moment you stop treating yourself as just a florist and start operating as a **business leader**, everything changes. You build a business that works for you—not the other way around.

> A SUCCESSFUL FLORAL BUSINESS ISN'T BUILT ON DOING EVERYTHING—IT'S BUILT ON LEADING WITH VISION AND STRATEGY.

What's Next...

In the next chapter, we'll explore **Systematizing Your Floral Business – The Key to Long-Term Success.** Get ready to future-proof your floral empire!

10

SYSTEMATIZING YOUR FLORAL BUSINESS – THE KEY TO LONG-TERM SUCCESS

I n the last chapter, we explored the importance of stepping into your role as a CEO and learning how to lead effectively. But leadership alone isn't enough—you need **systems** in place to ensure your business runs efficiently without constant oversight. This chapter will guide you through the process of systematizing your floral business, so it operates smoothly whether you're hands-on or stepping away.

A Business Without Systems is a Business That Owns You

Many floral entrepreneurs feel overwhelmed because they try to keep everything in their heads. They make pricing decisions on the spot, answer customer inquiries manually, and reinvent the wheel with every new client.

The problem? **Lack of systems leads to burnout, inefficiency, and lost revenue.**

Florists who implement strong business systems:

- Free up time to focus on creativity and growth.

- Provide a seamless experience for customers and employees.
- Reduce costly mistakes and increase profitability.
- Build a business that can operate even when they take time off.

Let's break down how you can build **scalable systems** that support your floral business for years to come.

My Turning Point With Business Systems

For a long time, I wore "busy" like a badge of honor.

If I wasn't physically in the shop, I was glued to my phone answering inquiries. I'd manually price every order, respond to every email, and constantly re-create proposals from scratch. My brain never shut off because *everything* lived in my head. I thought that was just what being a business owner meant—constant motion, constant stress.

But the truth? I was drowning in details.

One day, I forgot to send a final payment reminder to a wedding client. Not only did I deliver the flowers without being paid in full—I spent hours chasing the invoice afterward. That was my wake-up call.

So I made a commitment to myself:

No more building a business that collapses without me.

I started small:

- I created templates for pricing and proposals.
- I automated client follow-ups so I wasn't rewriting the same emails over and over.
- I documented how I wanted things done—from flower prep to delivery—to train new team members without hovering.

The difference was night and day.

Not only did I gain back hours each week—I finally had the clarity and space to focus on *growth* instead of survival. My business became smoother, more profitable, and far less reliant on me showing up for every single task.

That's the power of systems. And if you've been carrying your whole business on your back—I promise, you don't have to.

Building Scalable Systems for Floral Business

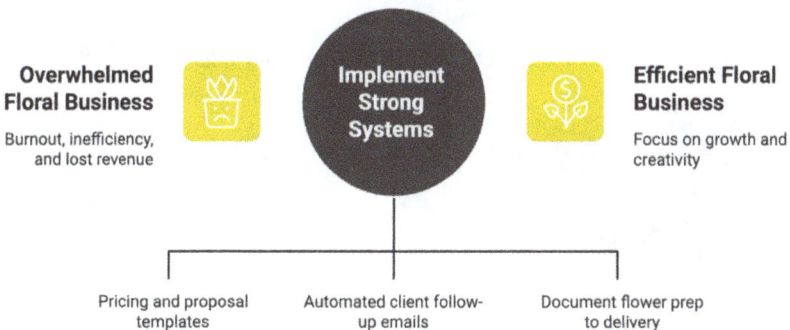

Overwhelmed Floral Business
Burnout, inefficiency, and lost revenue

Implement Strong Systems

Efficient Floral Business
Focus on growth and creativity

Pricing and proposal templates

Automated client follow-up emails

Document flower prep to delivery

Why Some Florists Stay Stuck While Others Scale Effortlessly

Let's compare two florists with the same level of talent:

Florist A: The Disorganized Business Owner

- Customizes every order manually and struggles to stay on top of inquiries.
- Feels like there's never enough time to work on growing the business.
- Spends hours fixing mistakes caused by lack of structure.
- Is afraid to step away because the business **can't run without them.**

Florist B: The Systematized Floral CEO

- Has standardized workflows for pricing, client onboarding, and order fulfillment.
- Uses automation to handle repetitive tasks.
- Delegates work confidently because there are **clear processes** in place.
- Can step away for vacations or emergencies without stress.

Which florist do you want to be?

Choose the best approach for managing a floral business

Disorganized Florist
Struggles with manual processes and lack of structure

Systematized Florist
Uses automation and clear processes for efficiency

Case Study: How Maria Gained Back 20 Hours a Week with Systems

Maria was known in her city for beautifully curated floral installations for corporate clients. But behind the scenes? She was barely holding it together.

She was:

- Quoting every job manually with different pricing each time.
- Responding to last-minute changes at all hours of the day.
- Forgetting to follow up with potential leads because they got lost in her inbox.

Her stress levels were high, and she wasn't making nearly enough to justify the chaos. What changed it all?

She decided to stop winging it and start systematizing.

- She built a **pricing matrix** that covered the most common floral configurations and delivery zones—so no more guessing or undercharging.
- She started using **HoneyBook** to automate her entire booking pipeline: inquiries, proposal templates, contracts, and payments.
- She developed a **service menu** with visual examples of her standard packages, which made her booking process smoother and easier for clients.

Within 6 months:

- She gained back 20 hours per week.
- Her conversion rate doubled because her proposals looked polished and professional.
- She increased her average order value by 30%—because the system gave clients clarity and confidence.

Takeaway: The more structure Maria created, the more freedom she had to focus on creativity and client experience.

Case Study: How Sasha Built a Self-Sufficient Wedding Business

Sasha was a beloved wedding florist in Seattle with a strong personal brand—but she was stuck.

Every wedding relied on *her*:

- Her eye for design.
- Her presence at every setup.
- Her brain for client details.

She loved her work, but it left no space for life outside it. No vacations. No weekends. No true downtime.

So she took a bold step:

She decided to build a business that didn't need her at every touchpoint.

- She created a **floral brand guide**—a document that detailed her go-to color palettes, texture preferences, vessel types, and "design philosophy." This became the blueprint for her team.
- She built a **workflow board** in Trello that showed every step of a wedding project—from inquiry to final strike—so her assistant could manage projects without asking her 20 questions a day.
- She automated **payment reminders** and added deadlines for approvals, eliminating back-and-forth emails and last-minute fire drills.

What happened?

- Her team executed weddings that matched her vision—without her direct involvement.
- She reduced her hours to 10–15 a week *by choice*—while maintaining quality and income.
- She had time to plan a vacation for the first time in three years.

Takeaway: Sasha didn't just systematize her business—she reclaimed her life.

The 5 Core Systems Every Florist Needs

1. Systematizing Your Pricing & Proposals

Pricing by "gut feeling" or adjusting prices on the fly leads to inconsistency and lost profit. Instead, create a **clear pricing system** that ensures profitability and efficiency.

- Develop a **pricing sheet** for standard arrangements and event packages.
- Use software like **Curate, Details Flowers, or True Client Pro** to generate quotes instantly.
- Train your team on pricing formulas so everyone follows the same structure.

Action Step: Create a standardized pricing guide for your business.

2. Automating Customer Communication & Inquiries

Florists spend hours answering the same questions from clients. Automate these responses to **save time and improve customer experience.**

- Use **chatbots and auto-responders** for common inquiries (pricing, availability, flower care tips).
- Set up **email automation** for follow-ups, invoices, and appointment reminders.
- Implement a **client portal** where customers can access order details.

Action Step: Draft a set of email templates for common client interactions (inquiries, follow-ups, thank-you messages).

3. Streamlining Order Fulfillment & Workflow

A business without a systemized order process is a **chaotic business.** Avoid last-minute rushes and missed details by setting up a **step-by-step workflow for fulfilling orders.**

- Use a **production schedule** so your team knows when to prep, arrange, and deliver.
- Implement **checklists** for quality control before orders leave the shop.
- Use digital tools like **Trello, Asana, or Monday.com** to track projects and deadlines.

Action Step: Create a simple checklist that outlines each stage of order fulfillment.

4. Building Opportunity and Performance Drivers for Delegation

If your team relies on you for every small decision, your business can't scale. Instead of focusing solely on traditional training manuals, build **Opportunity & Performance Drivers**—repeatable systems that drive results without constant micromanagement.

- Design **Opportunity Drivers** to bring in consistent revenue without your constant involvement (e.g., automated lead generation, referral programs, strategic partnerships).
- Develop **Performance Drivers** to ensure smooth operations, including documented workflows, automated order processing, and defined customer service protocols.
- Empower your team to **own** key aspects of the business by giving them clear outcomes and structured systems, instead of just task-based training.

Action Step: Identify one key area in your business that needs an Opportunity or Performance Driver. Map out the essential steps and begin implementing the system.

5. Managing Finances & Tracking Profitability

Without proper financial systems, even a busy floral business can struggle to stay profitable. **Know your numbers.**

- Use accounting software like **QuickBooks or Wave** to track expenses and revenue.
- Set up a **cash flow management system** to ensure steady income during slow months.
- Regularly review profit margins to adjust pricing and expenses.

Action Step: Schedule a monthly financial review to analyze profitability.

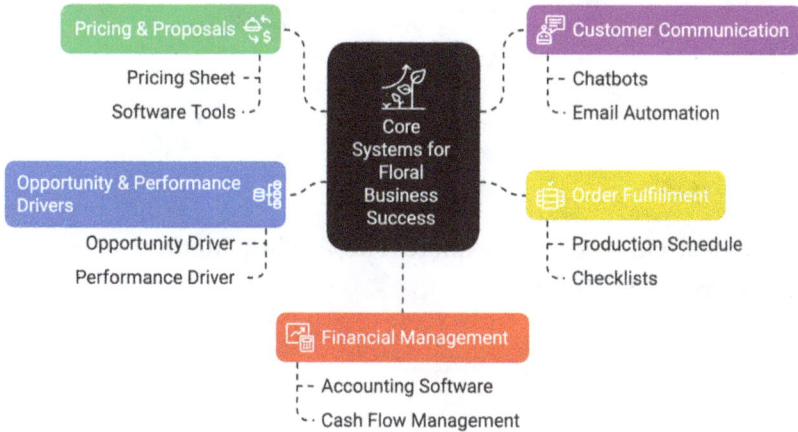

Core Systems for Floral Business Success

Bonus Tip: Test Your Systems by Taking a Step Back

A great way to see if your systems work is to **step away for a few days** and observe how well your business runs without you. If there are breakdowns, refine your systems accordingly.

- Take a weekend off and see how your team handles operations.
- Set up automated workflows and test them for efficiency.
- Identify weak spots and improve them before scaling further.

Systems Create Freedom

Systematizing your business isn't about losing creativity—it's about **gaining control** and **long-term sustainability**.

> A BUSINESS WITHOUT
> SYSTEMS IS A JOB.
> A BUSINESS WITH SYSTEMS
> IS A COMPANY.

What's Next...

In the next chapter, we'll explore **The Anchor Method - Creating Clients for Life.**

11

THE ANCHOR METHOD – CREATING CLIENTS FOR LIFE

I n Chapter 10, we explored the power of systematization—how creating processes allows your floral business to run smoothly without you. But building a successful business isn't just about operations. It's also about **relationships.** That's where **The Anchor Method** comes in—a system I developed to cultivate deep trust, repeat business, and long-term client loyalty.

In this chapter, we'll unpack my signature **Anchor Method,** which is more than a retention strategy—it's a framework for becoming **irreplaceable** to your clients. The best part? This method works whether you're a solo florist, running a team, or scaling up.

Loyalty Doesn't Happen by Accident—It Happens by Design

Many florists focus all their energy on getting new clients but neglect the goldmine in front of them: **past clients who already trust them.**

- It costs 5–7x more to acquire a new client than to retain an existing one.
- Loyal clients spend more, refer more, and are less price-sensitive.

- Retention allows you to **forecast revenue**, reduce stress, and build a business with stability.

Let's walk through how you can use the Anchor Method to **build meaningful, long-lasting client relationships that fuel your business.**

Why I Created the Anchor Method

When I first started my floral business, I used to believe that doing excellent work would be enough. That clients would naturally come back again and again simply because they loved their flowers. But time after time, I noticed something strange—my calendar stayed busy, but I was always chasing the next booking.

One weekend, after back-to-back weddings, I sat at my desk utterly exhausted. I pulled up my client list from the previous two years and realized that only a handful had ever rebooked or referred anyone. That moment hit me like a wave. **I was focused on performance, not partnership.**

So I began an experiment. What if I treated every client as if they were the beginning of a multi-year relationship, not a one-time event?

It started with one bride—Jenna. She was radiant, organized, and obsessed with florals. After her wedding, I didn't just say thank you. I sent a follow-up card and included a "just because" floral arrangement on her six-month anniversary. She was touched. That gesture led to designing her sister's wedding, a baby shower, and regular holiday decor for her home.

Over three years, Jenna's loyalty generated over **$18,000 in revenue**—but more than that, she became a brand evangelist, referring friends and posting about us constantly. All from a thoughtful moment and intentional follow-up.

This pattern repeated again and again. I documented what worked, refined it into a system, and realized I had created something powerful: **The Anchor Method.**

A repeatable process that:

- Increases retention and repeat bookings.
- Turns clients into referral machines.
- Positions you as the florist they can't imagine working without.

Now, it's a system I teach and implement in my business to this day. Let's dive in.

Building Client Loyalty with the Anchor Method

4 — Achieve Loyalty
Establish strong, lasting client relationships that drive repeat business.

3 — Implement the Method
Apply the system to build trust and loyalty with clients.

2 — Develop the Method
Create a system to foster long-term client relationships.

1 — Recognize the Need
Realize the importance of client retention over acquisition.

Why Most Florists Miss the Mark on Loyalty

Let's compare two florists who deliver beautiful designs:

Florist A: The Transactional Artist

- Books clients one event at a time.
- Doesn't follow up after delivery.
- Spends most of their time marketing to new people.
- Has inconsistent income and low client retention.

Florist B: The Trusted Anchor

- Builds deep, ongoing relationships with clients.
- Checks in before and after events.
- Creates systems for anniversaries, birthdays, and rebooking.
- Has a calendar full of repeat business and referrals.

Which one do you want to be?

Which florist model to adopt for sustainable business growth?

Transactional Artist VS **Trusted Anchor**

Focuses on one-time sales and new clients — Builds lasting relationships and repeat business

Case Study: From Occasional Orders to Ongoing Contracts

Lindsey, a florist in Georgia, had built a beautiful brand but was stuck in the feast-or-famine cycle. Her clients raved about her work, but they rarely came back. She joined my Anchor Method course and implemented the following:

- Created an onboarding guide that laid out expectations and timelines.
- Designed a celebration calendar that included client birthdays, anniversaries, and business milestones.
- Built a post-event follow-up sequence with handwritten thank-you notes and a subtle rebooking invitation.

One of her early Anchor clients was a couple who used her for their wedding. Lindsey sent them a first anniversary bouquet with a handwritten card referencing their wedding day florals. They were blown away.

That gesture led to a referral for the bride's sister's wedding, a baby shower, and eventually quarterly home floral deliveries.

Within six months:

- Lindsey booked **three recurring annual contracts** for corporate floral styling.
- Her average client value increased by 40%.
- 80% of her upcoming bookings came from **existing client relationships.**

She told me, "I used to feel like I had to constantly hustle for the next job. Now I feel like I'm building a garden that keeps blooming."

Let's break down how it works.

The 5 Anchors of Client Retention

The Anchor Method is built on **five core anchors**—pillars that create emotional connection, trust, and repeat engagement. Think of them as **touch-points that deepen loyalty** over time.

1. Anchor with Clarity

Clients trust what they understand. Set expectations clearly and early.

1. Outline what working with you looks like—from inquiry to delivery.
2. Share your process visually or in a short welcome video.
3. Include boundaries, timelines, communication preferences.

Action Step: Create a "What to Expect" document or page that walks clients through your process.

2. Anchor with Consistency

Consistency builds confidence.

- Use workflows and templates for all client communication.
- Deliver on your promises (and a little more).
- Keep branding and messaging aligned across platforms.

Action Step: Audit your emails and proposals. Are they consistent in tone, detail, and presentation?

3. Anchor with Celebration

Clients remember how you make them feel—especially when you celebrate them.

- Send a personal thank-you card or gift after a big event.
- Celebrate anniversaries, birthdays, or milestones.
- Acknowledge personal moments beyond business.

Action Step: Build a celebration calendar to track client events and send surprise touches.

4. Anchor with Continuity

Make the next step easy.

- Offer follow-up services or maintenance (ex: holiday décor, recurring deliveries).
- Mention rebooking in your final consultation.
- Create packages for ongoing engagement.

Action Step: Add a "next step" offer to your final client follow-up email.

5. Anchor with Connection

Connection creates community.

- Ask thoughtful questions that go beyond the transaction.
- Use your platform to spotlight client stories.

- Stay engaged on social media—comment, celebrate, support.

Action Step: Schedule time weekly to interact with past clients online or by message.

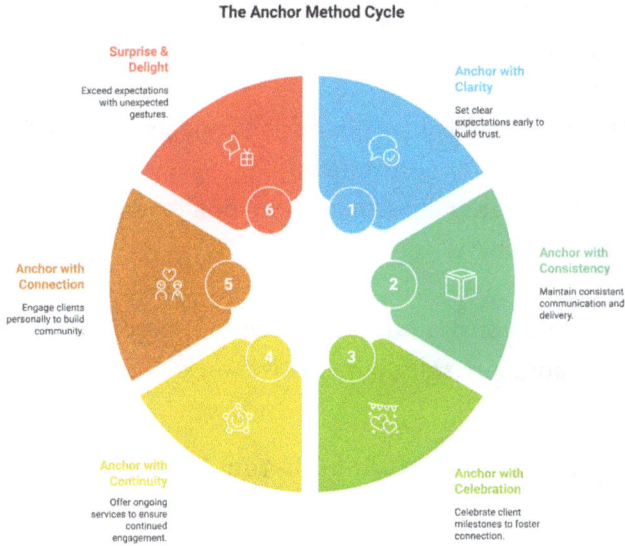

The Anchor Method Cycle

Surprise & Delight
Exceed expectations with unexpected gestures.

Anchor with Clarity
Set clear expectations early to build trust.

Anchor with Consistency
Maintain consistent communication and delivery.

Anchor with Connection
Engage clients personally to build community.

Anchor with Continuity
Offer ongoing services to ensure continued engagement.

Anchor with Celebration
Celebrate client milestones to foster connection.

Bonus Anchor: Surprise & Delight

People share what surprises them. Use this to your advantage.

- Include an unexpected gift in your delivery.
- Upgrade their experience with something they didn't expect.
- Remember small details (like their favorite flower or color).

Action Step: Choose one client this month to surprise in a meaningful way.

Turning the Anchor Method into a System

Retention isn't a task—it's a **system.** Here's how to turn these anchors into habits:

- Create a retention workflow in your CRM or project management tool.
- Assign anchor-related tasks to your team or automate them.
- Review your client list quarterly to update notes and look for rebooking opportunities.
- Use email campaigns and automation to nurture clients post-project.

When used consistently, this method becomes **a retention engine** that runs alongside your creative work.

How The Anchor Method Supports Your Scaling Goals

Client retention isn't just about good vibes—it's **smart business.**

- It reduces your marketing costs dramatically.
- It increases your average customer lifetime value.
- It creates predictability in your calendar and cash flow.
- It builds brand evangelists who refer their friends, family, and colleagues.

If you want to scale with stability and soul, mastering retention through The Anchor Method is essential.

Loyalty Can Be Designed

The Anchor Method isn't just about doing "extra." It's about intentionally weaving connection, trust, and continuity into your client journey so that loyalty isn't accidental—it's built into your brand.

When you anchor your clients emotionally and experientially, they don't just come back. They become champions of your business.

> ❝
> LOYALTY ISN'T LUCK—
> IT'S LEADERSHIP.
> DESIGN IT WITH INTENTION,
> AND YOU'LL NEVER RUN OUT
> OF BUSINESS.
> ❞

What's Next...

Now that you've learned how to retain your dream clients, we'll move into **Financial Mastery & Sustainable Growth**, exploring how to make every dollar work harder for you and your business.

12

MAINTAINING A PROFITABLE FLORAL BUSINESS THROUGH SUSTAINABLE GROWTH & FINANCIAL MASTERY

We looked at how systematizing your floral business may increase productivity, free up time, and lay the groundwork for long-term success in the last chapter. We now address a topic that is equally important: **financial mastery.**

A gorgeous bouquet of flowers won't sustain your company; **sound financial management** will. What distinguishes successful business owners from struggling florists is an understanding of cash flow, profit margins, and long-term viability.

Profitability Is Not Just About Revenue

Many florists believe that their company is financially stable as long as they are planning events and making sales. However, revenue by itself does not equate to profitability; rather, your company's success is determined by its pricing strategy, cash flow management, and expenses.

Financially savvy florists: Establish prices that guarantee sustained profitability; Prevent financial shocks and efficiently handle sluggish seasons; Invest in expansion through astute money management. Instead of only existing, start a firm that generates riches.

Let's examine how you can manage the finances of your floral business and guarantee long-term success.

My Financial Mastery Turning Point

From the outside, my business appeared successful—sophisticated setups, weekends that were completely booked, and excellent customer feedback. But I was always worried about money behind the scenes.

Every time I checked my bank account, I felt lost. I didn't stop working. Customers were pleased. Things were happening. Why, then, did I feel like I was just barely making ends meet?

Lack of business wasn't the issue. It was a lack of *financial clarity*.

I didn't have a sound system for pricing. I failed to monitor my cash flow. Furthermore, I had no strategy in place for the inescapably slow seasons. Even though I was earning money, I wasn't retaining it.

When I started paying attention to my numbers, everything changed.

- I developed a pricing strategy that made sure every deal was lucrative.
- I began expecting slow months after monitoring my cash flow.
- I eliminated wasteful spending and established income targets that genuinely fit with my growth strategy and way of life.

The result?

Financial peace of mind. Predictable profits. The ability to make decisions based on strategy rather than survival was also a significant advantage.

Becoming an accountant is not the goal of financial skills. The goal is to become an empowered CEO who is fully aware of the company's current state and future direction.

Achieving Financial Mastery in Floral Business

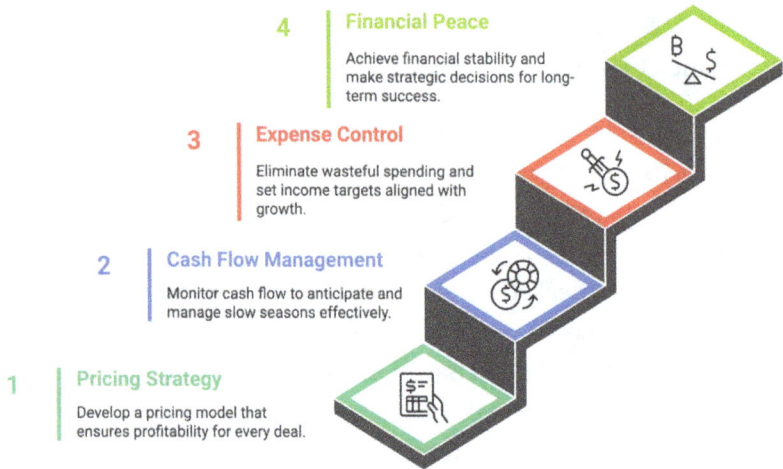

4 Financial Peace
Achieve financial stability and make strategic decisions for long-term success.

3 Expense Control
Eliminate wasteful spending and set income targets aligned with growth.

2 Cash Flow Management
Monitor cash flow to anticipate and manage slow seasons effectively.

1 Pricing Strategy
Develop a pricing model that ensures profitability for every deal.

Why Some Florists Fail While Others Build Wealth

Let's contrast two florists who are equally skilled and successful:

Florist A: The Owner of the Financially Struggling Business

- Bases prices on competitors' rates rather than profit margins.
- Has cash flow problems when business is slow.
- Has trouble with taxes and doesn't keep a tight eye on business spending.
- Feels anxious about money even though they have a full schedule.

Florist B: The Financially Savvy Floral CEO

- Makes sure each order is profitable by using a cost-plus pricing approach.
- Manages cash flow all year long using a seasonal financial plan.

- Makes investments in company expansion without taking on unnecessary debt.
- Manages a steady, financially stress-free company.

Which florist are you interested in becoming?

Choose the best financial strategy for a floral business.

Florist A
Focus on competition and short-term gains

vs

Florist B
Focus on profitability and long-term growth

Case Study: How Michelle Boosted Revenue Without Increasing Prices

In Detroit, Michelle operated a small wedding floral shop. She appeared to be doing a fantastic job, as evidenced by her booked-out weekends, excellent client testimonials, and stunning work. But what was going on behind the scenes? Every time payroll rolled around, she was in a frenzy.

Even though she was scheduling expensive weddings, she occasionally ran out of money. Why? Because she *used intuition rather than math* to determine her prices.

This is what made all the difference:

- After sitting down to **examine each line item** in her expenses, including the cost of the flowers, the ribbon, and the labor involved in delivery, she discovered that her profit margin was quite small.
- She found that, simply "for safety," she was **over-ordering 15–20% more flowers** than she needed, costing her thousands of dollars in lost revenue.

- To guarantee that every deal met her profit goal, she put in place a **cost-plus pricing system**.
- In order to cover weaker months, she was able to save during peak months by creating a **seasonal cash flow plan**.

She didn't bring on any more customers. She didn't increase prices. She simply managed more deliberately and priced more wisely.

The result?

- Profit increased by 40% in a year.
- No more cash flow problems at the end of the month.
- Every time she accepted a project, she felt at ease.

Takeaway: You need better money systems, not more work.

Case Study 2: André Created Wealth by Adopting an Owner's Perspective

André, an Atlanta-based high-end event florist, was incredibly imaginative and frequently hired for lavish weddings and massive installations. He was aware that floristry by itself wouldn't provide him long-term prosperity or freedom, despite his rising fame.

Even if he wasn't creating every centerpiece personally, he still wanted to create a business that suited him.

Therefore, he transitioned from *florist to floral entrepreneur.*

- In order to convert one-time expenses into ongoing revenue, he made an investment in a variety of **rental inventory**, including exquisite vases, candelabras, and arches, which he could utilize for occasions.
- He started an **online floral design course** that generated consistent passive income by teaching his distinctive method of color theory and installation mechanics.
- By streamlining his product offers and negotiating better

pricing with his suppliers, he was able to **reduce costs by 20%** without compromising quality.

In just three years, André:

- Increased his net profit by over 50%.
- Diversified his sources of income to avoid relying on weekend activities.
- Provided him with a financial buffer that allowed him to breathe and take innovative chances.

Takeaway: Developing smart systems and scalable revenue sources, not working harder, creates wealth.

Understanding the Finances of Floral Businesses

1. Establishing Pricing to Ensure Profitability

You're playing a risky game if you base your service prices on what competitors charge. **Your pricing strategy should be determined by your profit and cost objectives.**

- Employ a cost-plus pricing strategy (flowers + labor + profit + overhead).
- To cover costs, make sure floral arrangements have a 65%–70% gross margin.
- Charge for your time; florists frequently undercharge for design work.

Action Step: Examine and modify your pricing strategy to ensure steady profitability.

2. Handling Cash Flow Competently

The income of a florist varies from year to year. Financial stress is easy to face if you don't have a solid cash flow plan.

- Predict seasonal declines and accumulate a buffer during slow months.
- Automate savings: Put aside 10–15% of earnings for unexpected business expenses.
- To ensure future reservations and steady revenue, use retainers or deposits.

Action Step: Make a cash flow forecast for the upcoming 12 months as an action item.

3. Keeping Personal and Business Funds Separate

A common error made by florists is to combine personal and business funds, which makes it challenging to keep track of spending and establish expansion plans.

- Create a business bank account and only use it for business-related costs.
- Instead of periodically taking money out of your revenue, pay yourself a wage.
- Use software such as Wave or QuickBooks to keep track of every transaction.

Action Step: Create a specific business account and begin dividing finances right away if you haven't already.

4. Reducing Expenses Without Compromising Quality

Being economical isn't the same as being strategic when it comes to saving money. By optimizing expenditures, **you can reduce costs without sacrificing quality.**

- Try to get better prices from **wholesalers** and place larger orders whenever you can.
- To save money on sourcing, **use seasonal flowers.** Determine the **tools/products or subscription services** you are paying for but aren't using to their full potential. To cut down on transportation expenses, assess delivery logistics.

Action Step: This month, audit your spending and cut out at least one unneeded expense.

5. Creating Several Revenue Streams

Do you want to become more financially stable? **Diversify your revenue** sources rather than depending on just one.

- Provide local companies or corporate clientele with **subscription services.**
- Offer **online design guidance, digital courses, and flower workshops.**
- To obtain recurring contracts, collaborate with **interior designers or event planners.**
- To create passive income, spend money on rental décor.

Action Step: Within the next ninety days, choose one new source of income and begin testing it.

Top Strategies for Floral Business Success

Cost-Plus Pricing
Implement cost-plus pricing for consistent profitability.

Cash Flow Management
Manage cash flow effectively with seasonal planning.

Revenue Diversification
Diversify revenue streams for financial stability.

Bonus Tip: Before You Think You Need a Bookkeeper, Hire One

Hiring a bookkeeper is one of the best business investments you can make.

They will assist you in:

- Accurately tracking your finances to prevent tax shocks;
- Finding places to increase profitability;
- Freeing up your time to concentrate on expansion;
- Ensuring tax compliance and avoiding costly errors.

Action Step: This month, set up a consultation with a bookkeeper if you don't already have one.

Freedom Is Created by Financial Mastery

Building a **successful, long-lasting, and stress-free** flower business is the goal of financial mastery, not fussing over spreadsheets. You can concentrate on what you really love—designing, developing, and making an impact—when your finances are in order.

Growth Hacks:

1. The Bloom Budget Multiplier

Optimize your stem selections, batch labor, and streamline packaging to quietly boost profitability on your best-selling items without raising prices.

Why it works: Attempting to over-deliver their most popular designs causes most florists to lose money. They become subtly more profitable as a result.

2. The Slow Season Stash System

Put 10–15% of your highest-volume revenue into a special "Winter Bloom" bank account automatically. To maintain commitment, give it an emotional label, such as "Peace Fund."

Why it works: With time, you'll gain trust in your financial flow and navigate through sluggish months without stress.

3. The Menu Makeover Method

Instead of using itemized lists, repackage your offers into floral experiences that are centered on moods *(Romantic Dinner Escape, Corporate Vibe Lift, etc.)*. Add an additional 10–15% margin.

Why it works: Customers are more interested in the emotional result than the math, which makes it simpler to charge more without encountering any opposition.

4. The Lazy Luxury Add-On

At checkout, include high-profit extras like eco-wrap packaging, a soy candle, or a handwritten poem.

Why it works: It boosts the average order with minimal effort and appeals to consumers' desire to personalize their gifts.

5. The $1K Day Audit

Take a look at your most successful day ever. Analyze the sources of each dollar and the factors that contributed to the largest margin. Next, make a weekly schedule that follows the same format.

Why it works: You identify the offerings, customers, or services that really make a difference and begin constructing your company around them.

> A THRIVING FLORAL BUSINESS ISN'T JUST ABOUT SELLING MORE—IT'S ABOUT MANAGING MONEY WISELY AND GROWING WITH PURPOSE.

What's Next...

We'll talk about how to leave day-to-day operations and establish a flower business that can function without you in the upcoming chapter, **Exit Strategy – Preparing to Step Away.**

13

EXIT STRATEGY – PREPARING TO
STEP AWAY

In the last chapter, we covered **financial mastery** and how to ensure your floral business remains profitable and sustainable. Now, we take the next step: **designing an exit strategy** that allows you to step away while your business continues to thrive.

Many florists believe they must always be involved in every aspect of their business. But the ultimate goal of entrepreneurship is to create a business that can run **without being completely dependent on you.** Whether you want to retire, sell your business, or simply reduce your day-to-day involvement, having a well-thought-out **exit strategy** is essential.

A Business with an Exit Plan Has More Value

A business that relies entirely on its owner **has no long-term value.** But a business with systems, leadership, and a clear transition plan becomes an **asset** that can be sold, passed down, or even franchised.

Florists who plan their exit strategy:

- Increase the value of their business.
- Create a business that operates smoothly without them.

- Avoid burnout and enjoy more freedom.
- Have multiple options for transitioning out of daily operations.

Let's break down how to prepare your business for your eventual step back.

Why I Started Thinking About My Own Exit Strategy

When I first opened my floral business, the thought of stepping away never crossed my mind.

I was *the business*—the face, the designer, the decision-maker, the problem-solver. I built it from scratch with my own two hands. Letting go of that, even a little, felt impossible. And honestly, it felt unnecessary... until I realized how deeply my life was tied to the shop.

If I got sick? The business stalled.

If I needed a break? It wasn't happening.

If I ever wanted to slow down or do something different? There was no plan.

That realization hit hard: I hadn't built a business—I'd built a beautiful cage.

That's when I started asking different questions:

- What would happen if I needed to take a month off?
- What would it look like to have *options*—to scale back, sell, or shift into mentorship?
- How do I create a business that works *for me*, instead of one that only works *because of me*?

The answers led me to my exit strategy—not because I was done, but because I wanted to build something that could live, grow, and thrive beyond just *me.*

That shift didn't just give me peace of mind. It gave me freedom.

Designing a Floral Business Exit Strategy

Why Some Florists Burn Out While Others Build Legacy Businesses

Let's compare two florists who have built successful businesses:
Florist A: The Burned-Out Business Owner

- Still handles most of the daily operations personally.
- Has no team that can run the business without them.
- Feels overwhelmed and unable to take vacations or step away.
- When they stop working, the business stops generating revenue.

Florist B: The Floral Entrepreneur with an Exit Plan

- Has built a **team and leadership structure** to handle daily operations.
- Has **documented systems and workflows** so the business runs smoothly.
- Can take vacations or even retire without the business failing.
- Has a **sellable asset** if they ever decide to exit completely.

Which florist do you want to be?

Which business model to adopt for long-term success and personal freedom?

Burned-Out Business Owner
Leads to personal exhaustion and business stagnation

Floral Entrepreneur with Exit Plan
Enables personal freedom and business growth

Case Study: Lena's Transition to Semi-Retirement

Lena built a thriving floral studio in Florida with a reputation for elegant, timeless arrangements. Her community adored her. Her clients trusted her. Her brand was strong. But after two decades of weddings, events, and daily deliveries—she was ready for something more: travel, family time, and rest.

At first, the idea of stepping away terrified her. Her name was the brand. Her touch was on everything. But deep down, she knew she had built something worth preserving—and that meant preparing it to exist without her.

So she began her transition:

- She hired a **General Manager** to oversee daily operations. Instead of jumping in to fix every issue, she empowered her GM to make decisions.
- She created a **40-page operations manual**, documenting how orders were taken, processed, fulfilled, and delivered —down to the way the ribbons were tied.
- She moved into a **consultant role**, reviewing marketing, finances, and design strategy just a few hours a week.

Today, Lena checks in once or twice a week from her beach condo or a coffee shop. Her business continues to grow. Her team feels empowered. And she's proof that stepping back doesn't mean letting go of your legacy—it means *protecting it*.

Takeaway: A semi-retirement plan can give you space to enjoy your life *without* sacrificing the success of your business.

Case Study: Mark's Profitable Exit Through Strategic Sale

Mark, a floral entrepreneur in Colorado Springs, had built a well-known floral business serving luxury weddings and high-end events. But after years of intense growth, he felt a pull to do something different—maybe write, maybe teach, maybe just breathe. He didn't want to shut down the business, but he *did* want out of the day-to-day.

Instead of burning out or walking away, Mark made a plan.

- He **streamlined his financial records**, working with a bookkeeper to organize every dollar earned and spent over the past three years.
- He **strengthened client contracts** to create reliable, recurring revenue that would look appealing to a buyer.
- He documented every major system—proposal process, flower sourcing, staff roles, and design templates—so a new owner wouldn't have to guess.
- He partnered with a **business broker** who specialized in creative brands and positioned his business as a high-value, high-potential investment.

The result?

Multiple interested buyers.

One of them—a design-focused entrepreneur looking to expand into florals—bought Mark's business for a strong six-figure offer.

Now, Mark teaches workshops, consults for florists, and spends his weekends exploring the Texas hill country with his camera instead of prepping flower buckets.

Takeaway: If you build your business with intention, selling it can be not just possible—but *profitable.*

Steps to a Smooth Exit Strategy

1. Systematize Your Business for Independence

Before you step away, your business must be **capable of running without you.**

- Create your **Opportunity & Performance Drivers or SOPs (Standard Operating Procedures)** for key tasks.
- Train your team to handle **sales, operations, and customer service.**
- Use automation for **invoicing, marketing, and customer follow-ups.**
- Document vendor relationships to ensure continuity after you step away.

Action Step: Document your daily tasks and delegate at least one major responsibility this month.

2. Identify & Train Your Successor

If you plan to step away, you need a **trusted leader or team** to take over.

- Identify a **key employee** who can take on more responsibility.
- Start **mentoring and empowering** them to make decisions.
- Provide leadership training to ensure they are fully prepared.
- Establish a **timeline** for transitioning leadership.

Action Step: Choose one person in your business to start training for a leadership role.

3. Choose Your Ideal Exit Strategy

There are several ways to transition out of your business—pick the one that fits your goals:

✔ **Selling the Business:** Find a buyer (another florist, an investor, or a franchise group).

✔ **Passing It Down:** Train a family member or trusted employee to take over.

✔ **Franchising or Licensing:** Expand your brand by allowing others to operate under your name.

✔ **Stepping Into a Consultant Role:** Stay involved but reduce your hours and responsibilities.

✔ **Creating a Passive Income Model:** Generate income through online courses, books, or brand licensing.

Action Step: Write down which exit strategy aligns best with your long-term vision.

4. Prepare Your Business for Sale (If Selling Is Your Goal)

If you want to sell your business, it must be **attractive to buyers.**

- Have **clear financial records** showing profitability.
- Ensure **all operations are systemized** and not reliant on you.
- Strengthen your **brand reputation and client contracts** for stability.
- Work with a **business broker** to properly value and market your business.

Action Step: Meet with a business broker to understand the valuation of your floral company.

5. Create Passive Income Streams for Ongoing Revenue

Even after stepping away, you can still **generate income** from your expertise.

- Offer **online floral courses** or a membership community.
- License your floral brand or design methods.
- Create an **investment strategy** using profits from your business.
- Sell digital products like floral guides, templates, or design blueprints.

Action Step: Brainstorm one passive income stream that aligns with your expertise.

Steps to a Profitable Business Exit

5 — **Create Passive Income** — Develop ongoing revenue streams post-exit.

4 — **Prepare for Sale** — Ensure financial clarity and brand strength for buyers.

3 — **Choose Exit Strategy** — Select the best transition method for your goals.

2 — **Identify Successor** — Mentor and empower a key employee for leadership.

1 — **Systematize Business** — Create SOPs and train staff for independence.

Bonus Tip: Test Your Exit Plan Before Fully Stepping Away

Before you completely step back, **run a test.**

- Take a **month-long break** and let your team run the business.
- Evaluate what worked and where improvements are needed.
- Make final adjustments before fully transitioning.
- Conduct a **stress test** by simulating your absence and measuring results.

Action Step: Plan a short leave and assess how well your business operates without you.

What This All Means: Your Business Should Work for You—Not the Other Way Around

Having an exit strategy isn't about quitting—it's about **building a business that works without your constant involvement.**

- If you want to sell, your business should be **a valuable, independent asset.**
- If you want to step back, **your team and systems should run the business.**
- If you want financial freedom, your **business should generate wealth beyond your daily labor.**

> " A TRULY SUCCESSFUL BUSINESS IS ONE THAT CAN THRIVE EVEN WHEN ITS FOUNDER STEPS AWAY. "

What's Next...

In the next chapter, we'll explore **Building a Lasting Floral Legacy—How to Ensure Your Impact Lives On,** whether through mentorship, brand expansion, or industry innovation!

14

CREATING A LASTING FLORAL LEGACY: MAKING SURE YOUR INFLUENCE CONTINUES AFTER YOU'VE GONE

We covered how to create an **exit strategy** in the last chapter so that your flower business can prosper without your day-to-day involvement. We now go on to a more significant query: **What sort of legacy are you hoping to leave behind?**

In addition to managing a company, a true flower entrepreneur **inspires others, shapes an industry, and leaves a lasting impression.** Your impact can go beyond your professional life, whether your goal is to mentor, build a well-known brand, or innovate in the floristry industry.

Impact, Not Just Income, Builds Legacy

It's simple to concentrate just on growth and profits, but the people you influence and the impression you make establish your legacy.

Inspiring and mentoring upcoming floral entrepreneurs; creating businesses that outlive them and continue to thrive; innovating and setting new standards in floral design and business practices; and giving back to their communities through sustainability initiatives, education, or philanthropy are all examples of florists who leave a lasting legacy. are renowned for their leadership, artistic abilities, and industry accomplishments.

Let's look at creating a floral legacy that leaves a lasting impression.

How I Started Considering My Own Legacy

At first, legacy wasn't something I considered.

Making rent, scheduling weddings, and establishing a reputation were my main priorities at the time. Gaining the next customer, event, or "wow" moment was the measure of success. After years of developing my business, coaching my staff, and working with amazing clients, I eventually started to ask myself a more important question:

What will happen when I'm not the one with the floral knife anymore?

I came to see that I had created influence in addition to a business. They were copying my techniques. Trends were being set by my approach to floral business. And in addition to complimenting my design work, florists were contacting me to inquire about how I developed my business.

It dawned on me then:

People, not petals and stems, would be the actual measure of my legacy.

The people I coached. The structure that I helped create. The information I imparted enabled someone else to realize their ambition.

The instant you begin to consider what you're creating for others rather than just for yourself, you're beginning to leave your floral legacy.

Building a Floral Legacy

Initial Focus — Just making rent payments

Business Growth — Develop business and coach staff

Industry Influence — Techniques copied, trends being set

Mentoring Others — Coaching and sharing information

Lasting Legacy — Impact beyond petals and stems

Why Some Florists Fade Away While Others Leave an Industry-Wide Impact

Let's contrast two florists with prosperous careers:

Florist A: The Short-Term Thinker

- Solely concentrates on reservations and quick earnings.
- Doesn't teach future leaders or record their procedures.
- Avoids spending money on connections or long-term branding.
- Their brand vanishes when they retire.

Florist B: The Legacy Builder

- Creates a lasting, powerful, and identifiable brand.
- Mentors and instructs aspiring florists.
- Creates a scalable company that can operate without them.
- Establishes new standards and trends, which benefits the industry.
- They are renowned for their impact, philanthropy, and inventiveness.

Which florist are you interested in becoming?

Choose the florist approach that aligns with your career goals.

Short-Term Thinker	VS	Legacy Builder
Focus on immediate gains and personal success		Focus on long-term impact and industry growth

Case Study: The Industry-Shaping Floral Icon

The Santa Fe-based luxury florist Camille had already established a hugely prosperous flower shop. Her earthy, sculptural, and intensely emotional arrangements were used in editorial spreads, upscale weddings, and art galleries all over the nation.

However, one afternoon after getting her tenth direct message of the week from a budding florist seeking guidance, she came to the crucial realization that her impact didn't have to stop with the subsequent flower. It might end up being her legacy.

She therefore made the decision to use her knowledge for a project greater than herself:

- She established a platform for online floral education that combined business coaching, floral philosophy, and creative instruction.
- In her book on conscious floristry and sustainable business, she discussed how to build a career that is based on both art and purpose.
- Additionally, she collaborated with global designers to promote floristry as a respected high art by organizing seasonal displays that conflate sculpture and nature.

These days, Camille's name is not only connected to exquisite work; it also connotes the advancement of the industry.

Takeaway: Being remembered is only one aspect of legacy. Redefining what is feasible for the upcoming generation is the goal.

Case Study 2: The Legacy Driven by the Community of Minneapolis-based floral designer James

James based his company on locally grown, in-season flowers and a strong feeling of community. His workshop eventually evolved into a center for **growth, education, and interaction** rather than merely a location to purchase flowers.

James didn't want to be famous when he started to consider his legacy. *Impact* was what he desired.

He then started giving each petal a purpose:

- He taught young people who had never thought of themselves as artists the fundamentals of flower design and entrepreneurship through monthly community workshops he held in underprivileged districts.
- Through his studio, he established a career training program that provides possibilities to individuals from atypical backgrounds or those returning to the industry.
- In order to recycle event flowers into bedside arrangements for hospitals, shelters, and assisted living facilities, he collaborated with nearby nonprofit organizations.
- Additionally, he shared the highs, lows, and genuine behind-the-scenes of being a mission-driven business owner in a free online diary that chronicled his journey.

James is semi-retired now, yet his studio still operates with the same passion as before. He is still discussed in his community as a *difference-maker* as well as a florist.

Takeaway: Legacy is about roots, not fame. Your influence will blossom long after you've moved on if you plant deep ones.

Crafting a Legacy That Lasts

1. Establish Your Legacy Objectives

What would you like to be known for? Making floral design a respected art form could be your legacy.

- Educating and mentoring other florists in order to empower them.
- Supporting environmentally friendly floristry techniques.
- Making a significant contribution to your community.
- Establishing oneself as an influential figure in the world of flowers.

Action Step: Put in writing the long-term effects you want your floral business to have.

2. Establish a Brand That Will Last

Beyond your direct engagement, your brand should be a recognizable identity that embodies **more than just you.**

- Create a distinctive floral design that people will identify with your name.
- Establish a solid web presence that details your ideology and work.
- Use licensing and trademarks to safeguard your brand.
- Create an environment at work that draws in bright people who share your beliefs.

Action Step: Create a brand vision statement that captures your long-term influence as an action item..

3. Guide and Educate the Upcoming Generation

Legacy is about what you leave behind, not just what you do.

- Provide training courses or apprenticeships to prospective florists.
- Conduct in-person training courses, webinars, or workshops.
- Provide a certification course for florists who wish to use your techniques.

- Train team members who will continue your job in leadership.

Action Step: Within the next six months, decide how you can begin teaching or mentoring.

4. Encourage Innovation in the Industry

Your name will become linked with advancement in floristry if you set new benchmarks and spearhead innovation.

- Try out **novel floral designs, materials, or technological advancements.**
- Share your knowledge by speaking at **industry conferences.**
- Collaborate with **academic institutions or research centers** to promote floristry.
- Create environmentally friendly floristry methods that are sustainable.

Action Step: Decide which industry trend or problem you wish to assist in resolving.

5. Develop a Philanthropic Arm and Give Back

Businesses that give back are often the most remembered. Think about:

- Funding **scholarships for flower design.**
- Giving **flowers to shelters, hospitals, or neighborhood gatherings.**
- Collaborating with **charitable organizations that promote sustainability in floristry.**
- Endorsing mental health programs for flower industry entrepreneurs.

Action Step: Pick a cause and incorporate it into your company plan.

6. Record Your Expertise for Upcoming Generations

Because it is documented and disseminated, a genuine legacy endures.

- Compose a book or an online manual about flower design or business.
- To share insights, start a YouTube channel, podcast, or blog.
- Create a floral entrepreneurship online course.
- Establish a florists' association or resource center.

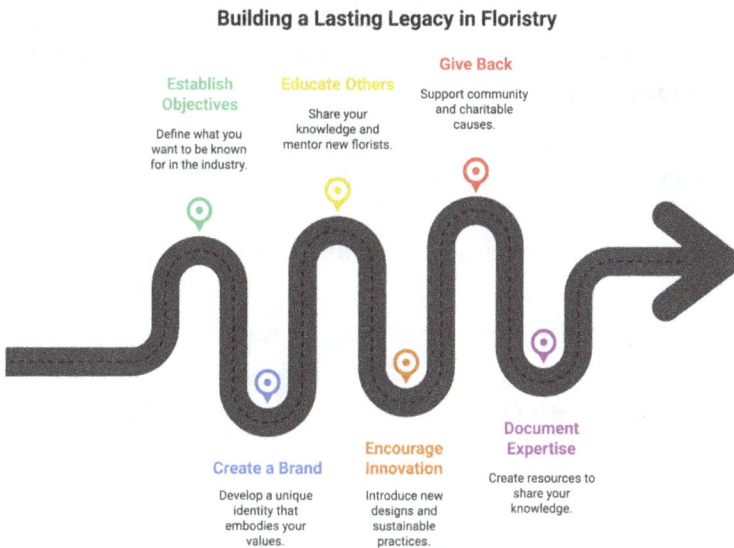

Building a Lasting Legacy in Floristry

Establish Objectives
Define what you want to be known for in the industry.

Educate Others
Share your knowledge and mentor new florists.

Give Back
Support community and charitable causes.

Create a Brand
Develop a unique identity that embodies your values.

Encourage Innovation
Introduce new designs and sustainable practices.

Document Expertise
Create resources to share your knowledge.

Action Step: Outline a piece of instructional material you could begin creating.

BONUS TIP: **Include Your Community in Your Legacy Plan**

Including people in your journey will increase your effect. Think about:

- Creating a network of floral experts who share your interests.

- Holding a yearly networking event or summit for the floral industry.
- Promoting cooperation over rivalry.
- Mentoring up-and-coming florists and newbies to the field.

Action Step: Look for a method to interact with the floral community in your area or online.

Your Influence May Last Longer Than Your Life

Making a lasting impact on the flower industry for **future generations is more important than ego.**

- Document and share your expertise if you want your work to endure.
- Establish new norms and trends if you wish to have an impact on the sector.
- Mentor, invent, and give back if you want to change the world.
- Create something greater than yourself if you want people to remember you.

> A TRUE FLORAL LEGACY ISN'T JUST ABOUT FLOWERS—IT'S ABOUT THE LIVES YOU TOUCH AND THE INSPIRATION YOU LEAVE BEHIND.

What's Next...

In the next chapter, we'll explore **The Grand Finale – What's Next for You and Your Floral Business?.**

15

THE GRAND FINALE – WHAT'S NEXT FOR YOU AND YOUR FLORAL BUSINESS?

We covered how to create a **lasting floral legacy that goes beyond your company** in the last chapter. Now, we arrive at the grand finale of this journey—**what's next for you?**

Building a floral business isn't just about flowers—it's about crafting a **fulfilling, profitable, and impactful** career. Whether you are just starting, scaling, or preparing for long-term success, the choices you make today will shape your future.

This chapter will help you create a clear **vision and action plan** to move forward with confidence, ensuring that your business aligns with your personal goals, financial ambitions, and legacy.

Your Business Should Serve Your Life—Not the Other Way Around

The most successful floral entrepreneurs design their businesses **around their ideal lifestyles.** They don't just work for the sake of working; they create businesses that support their financial goals, passions, and personal freedom.

Florists who thrive long-term:

- Know what success looks like for them personally and professionally.
- Regularly assess and adjust their business strategy.
- Balance **passion with profitability.**
- Take intentional steps toward scaling, diversifying, or stepping back when ready.
- Invest in professional and personal growth to sustain long-term success.

Cycle of Floral Business Success

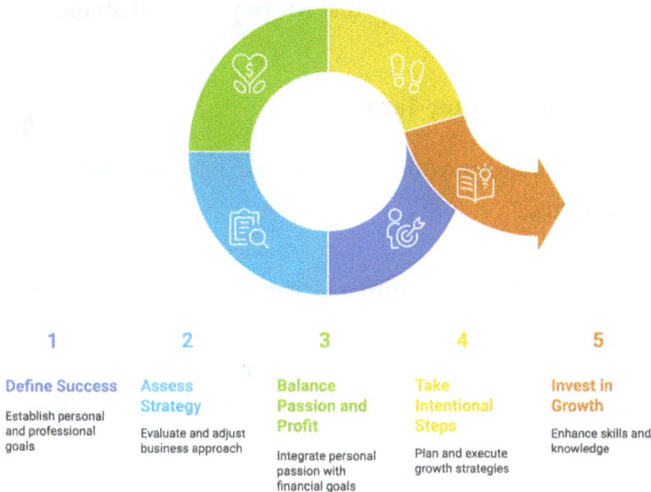

1	2	3	4	5
Define Success	**Assess Strategy**	**Balance Passion and Profit**	**Take Intentional Steps**	**Invest in Growth**
Establish personal and professional goals	Evaluate and adjust business approach	Integrate personal passion with financial goals	Plan and execute growth strategies	Enhance skills and knowledge

How I Transformed My Own Future

At one point in my business, I felt like I was **working non-stop but not making real progress.** I realized that I needed to ask myself important questions:

- Was my business model sustainable?
- Did my daily tasks align with my long-term goals?
- Was I working harder instead of working smarter?
- Was I prioritizing profitability as much as creativity?

Once I took control of my vision, I:

- Focused on **high-profit offerings** and let go of low-value services.
- Created **systems and automation** to free up my time.
- Set financial targets that aligned with the lifestyle I wanted.
- Created an **investment plan** to ensure financial security for the future.

Now, let's help you **define and achieve** your next steps.

Step 1: Clarify Your Long-Term Vision

The first step in shaping your future is asking, **where do you want to be in 5 or 10 years?**

- Do you want to grow into a larger floral empire or stay boutique-sized?
- Do you want to **scale, automate, or step back?**
- Are you interested in **mentoring, teaching, or writing a book?**
- Would you like to expand into **e-commerce, digital products, or speaking engagements?**
- Do you want to **invest in other businesses or real estate to diversify income?**

Action Step: Write down your **ideal future scenario** for your floral business and lifestyle.

Step 2: Align Your Business Model with Your Goals

Your business model should match your ambitions and desired lifestyle.

- If you want **financial growth**, focus on **scalable revenue streams** like subscriptions or courses.
- If you want **creative freedom**, build a brand that allows for artistic exploration.
- If you want **more time off**, develop a team and operational systems that support passive income.
- If you want **industry impact**, invest in thought leadership, speaking, or community initiatives.
- If you want **long-term wealth**, develop a diversified investment strategy.

Action Step: Identify one change to make in your business that will move you closer to your ideal vision.

Step 3: Strengthen Your Financial Foundation

A strong financial foundation gives you the freedom to make bold moves.

- Set **clear revenue goals** that align with your desired lifestyle.
- Develop a **cash reserve strategy** for stability.
- Evaluate **profit margins** on all services and products.
- Plan for **retirement or long-term financial security.**
- Build an **investment portfolio** that allows your money to grow outside of your business.

Action Step: Review your financials and set 1-year, 3-year, and 5-year revenue goals.

Step 4: Future-Proof Your Business with Innovation

The best businesses evolve to **stay relevant** and **meet market demands.**

- Monitor **industry trends and technological advancements.**
- Continue **building your brand's authority and online presence.**
- Experiment with **new marketing strategies** and customer engagement tools.
- Explore **sustainability and eco-conscious business models.**
- Invest in **AI-driven automation** to optimize operations and marketing.

Action Step: Research an emerging trend and brainstorm how you can integrate it into your business.

Step 5: Design Your Exit Strategy (Even If It's Years Away)

At some point, you'll want to **step back, sell, or transition your business.** Planning ahead ensures that your company remains valuable and thriving beyond your personal involvement.

- Develop a **succession plan** to pass leadership to a trusted person.
- Systematize your business to make it **sellable or transferable.**
- Decide if you want to remain in a **consulting role** or exit completely.
- Document your processes and **strengthen your brand's value.**
- Consider licensing or franchising your business model.

Action Step: Outline your ideal exit strategy—even if it's 10 years away.

Future Planning for Floral Business

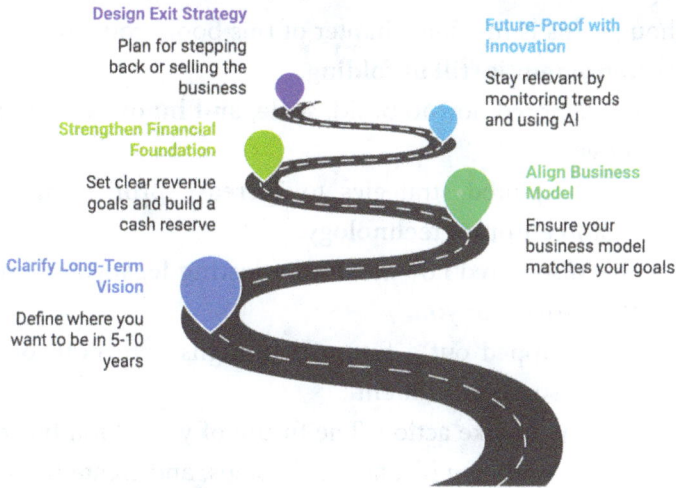

Design Exit Strategy

Plan for stepping back or selling the business

Strengthen Financial Foundation

Set clear revenue goals and build a cash reserve

Clarify Long-Term Vision

Define where you want to be in 5-10 years

Future-Proof with Innovation

Stay relevant by monitoring trends and using AI

Align Business Model

Ensure your business model matches your goals

Bonus Tip: Build a Support System for Continued Success

The best entrepreneurs surround themselves with **mentors, peers, and industry networks.**

- Join **florist mastermind groups or business coaching programs.**
- Build relationships with **other successful floral entrepreneurs.**
- Invest in **continued learning and professional development.**
- Stay accountable by setting quarterly business growth check-ins.
- Engage in **philanthropy or mentorship** to give back to the industry.

Action Step: Connect with at least one **mentor, coach, or industry leader** this year.

Final Thoughts: Your Journey is Just Beginning

Even though this is the final chapter of this book, **your journey as a floral entrepreneur is still unfolding.**

✅ You've learned how to **build, scale, and innovate** within your floral business.

✅ You've explored strategies to **increase profits, streamline operations, and embrace technology.**

✅ You've discovered how to **build a lasting legacy and create a business that works for you.**

✅ You've mapped out a future that aligns with both **business success and personal fulfillment.**

Now, it's time to take action. The future of your floral business is in your hands—so dream big, take bold steps, and create the success that you deserve.

> ❝ SUCCESS ISN'T ABOUT REACHING A DESTINATION— IT'S ABOUT CONTINUOUSLY GROWING, EVOLVING, AND BUILDING A BUSINESS THAT ALIGNS WITH YOUR BIGGEST DREAMS. ❞

What's Next?

This book may be ending, but your floral journey is just beginning. Now, go out and build the business—and the life—you've always envisioned!

If you have any questions, need further guidance, or want to connect, feel free to reach out at **info@propelbusinessadivors.com.** I'd love to hear about your journey and support you along the way! This book may be ending, but your floral journey is just beginning.

Now, go out and build the business—and the life—you've always envisioned!